'The subject of tidying first caught my attention when I was in junior high school. The catalyst was a book called *The Art of Discarding* by Nagisa Tatsumi, which explained the importance of getting rid of unnecessary things. . . . I can still remember the shock and surprise I felt as I read it on the train. I became so absorbed that I almost missed my stop. Once home, I went straight to my room with a handful of garbage bags and stayed closeted for several hours. Although the room was small, by the time I was finished I had eight bags full of stuff. . . . I had forgotten that most of these things even existed. I sat motionless on the floor for about an hour afterwards staring at the pile of bags and wondering, 'Why on earth did I bother keeping all this stuff?''

–Marie Kondo, *The Life-Changing Magic of Tidying*

THE ART
OF
DISCARDING

HOW TO GET
RID OF CLUTTER
AND FIND JOY

NAGISA TATSUMI

Translated by Angus Turvill

First published in Great Britain in 2017 by Yellow Kite
An imprint of Hodder & Stoughton
An Hachette UK company

First published in Japan with the title *Suteru! Gijutsu* by Takarajimasha, Inc.,
Tokyo, Japan.
English translation rights arranged with Takarajimasha, Inc. through
The English Agency (Japan) Ltd

A CIP catalogue record for this title is available from the British Library

Hardback ISBN 978 1 473 64821 0
Ebook ISBN 978 1 473 64822 7

Typeset in Optima 11/16.75 pt by
Palimpsest Book Production Limited, Falkirk, Stirlingshire

Printed and bound by CPI Group (UK) Ltd, Croydon CR0 4YY

Hodder & Stoughton policy is to use papers that are natural, renewable
and recyclable products and made from wood grown in sustainable
forests. The logging and manufacturing processes are expected to
conform to the environmental regulations of the country of origin.

Yellow Kite
Hodder & Stoughton Ltd
Carmelite House
50 Victoria Embankment
London EC4Y 0DZ

www.yellowkitebooks.co.uk

www.hodder.co.uk

Contents

Preface: Getting to grips with *stuff*   3

Introduction: What do you find
difficult to throw away and why?   15

Part One: You can master the art of discarding:
    Ten attitudes to help you get rid of things

  1: Don't keep it 'for now'   35

  2: Avoid 'temporary' storage – decide now! 42

  3: 'Sometime' never comes   48

  4: 'Really convenient!' to somebody
     else – irritating junk to me   54

  5: Nothing is sacred   60

  6: If you've got it, use it   66

  7: Storage and organisation methods
     are not the solution   71

  8: 'Maybe this could go . . .'   80

  9: Don't worry that you'll get rid of
     something you shouldn't   84

10: Don't aim for perfection   90

Part Two: Time to get rid of it:
Ten strategies for discarding

1: Don't look – throw!   97
2: Chuck it there and then   101
3: Discard when you exceed a certain
   amount   110
4: Discard after a certain period of time   115
5: Regular discarding   119
6: Discard things even if they can
   still be used   126
7: Establish discarding criteria   132
8: Have plenty of disposal routes   136
9: Start small   141
10: Who disposes of what? Decide
    responsibilities   146

Part Three: How to feel better about
getting rid of things:

Alternatives to throwing away   153

Afterword   165
About the author   167
About the translator   168

PREFACE

Getting to grips with *stuff*

Throwing stuff out: it's a fundamental issue.

Everyone these days has too much 'stuff'. We keep chucking it out, but it keeps on accumulating. At work, we face endless piles of paper; at home, however much storage space we have, it's never enough. Things proliferate and our living space shrinks. We're surrounded. We know we have to do something. If only we could get rid of it all, what a relief that would be!

The 1990s saw a boom in ecological thinking, which has extended into the new millennium: be kind to the Earth . . . Recycle . . . Don't produce rubbish . . . And this has generated a new way of thinking about stuff and what we *need* versus what we *want*. But we're still crowded out with it. Why? How come this flood of things never seems to ebb away?

We know how good it would feel if all this stuff was gone – so why we do we keep it? Why do we always feel guilty about getting rid of things? Let's look at these questions a little more closely.

STUFF AND OUR SENSE OF WASTE

In the past, things were precious. Before the start of mass production and mass consumption – relatively recently, in fact – things were cherished. They were looked after and used for as long as possible. Even when they'd lost their original purpose, other uses were found for them. And only once all possible functions were exhausted were they finally discarded. It was the same with food. People were taught to eat every last grain of rice in their bowls. It was all about using something to the full, discarding it and only then obtaining something new. That was the cycle and, against this background, a sense of shame at wastefulness (*mottainai* in Japanese) became a virtue.

But life's different now.

In the 1960s and 70s new and exciting electrical products sold precisely because they were new and exciting. There was a belief that new = good, and so things that were old were immediately replaced. More and more things – electrical goods, fashion, etc. – came flooding into our lives and, by the end of the 1980s, the act of purchasing had become an end in itself.

We've become used to this kind of spending, but because we are no longer buying out of necessity, things inevitably accumulate at a far greater pace than they are used up, and so we are drowning in stuff.

The switch from an era when things were precious to an era of over-supply was too sudden. We're stuck between our

4

traditional sense of wastefulness (*mottainai*) and the new world where things proliferate.

BE POSITIVE ABOUT DISCARDING

We have to address this dilemma. If we carry on like this, we'll never be free of the spell that things have over us.

Can a more ecologically aware or economical lifestyle help us break the spell? If we look after things and only buy what's necessary, will we be free? Well, it wouldn't work for me. I wouldn't want to stop buying things. Reducing clutter feels good, but you'd have to be very stoic to enjoy life without new stuff.

It feels good to have things you like around you. It makes you happy to wear new clothes. I have a TV and newspapers, but I want magazines too. If I want to buy some new plates or a jug, I don't want to be thinking there's something virtuous about preventing myself from doing so. Saving money's no good if you can't enjoy life.

So we want to enjoy a comfortable life, but we don't want things to accumulate; nor do we want to create a sense of waste. Is that possible? And, if so, how?

This book is here to help. What I want to propose is a positive attitude to discarding. To get to grips with our cluttered lives we have to start clearing things out. Instead of worrying about wastefulness, let the task of disposal be an opportunity to reflect on the real value of your possessions. Look at the things you've allowed to accumulate. Thinking about why you've got them will help give you a sense of why they have a hold on you. And as you sort out what to throw away and what to keep, you'll come to realise what's really necessary.

THE ART OF DISCARDING AND
THE ART OF LIVING

First off, you need to reassess your relationship with physical objects. The ten attitudes to discarding outlined in Part One will help you. I'm not saying you should change your mindset completely, but if you worry about throwing things away, perhaps it's time to adjust your thinking a little. Just try adopting the key points from this section that strike a chord with you. This may help loosen the hold that things have on you. Part Two introduces ten practical disposal strategies. As with Part One, try what makes sense to you. If just one of the strategies becomes a habit, life will start to feel much better. In Part Three, there's some general information that should make it easier for you to find ways to get rid of things. I hope you'll find it useful to combine this with suggestions from the other two parts.

You'll find a lot of detail in the book, but ultimately the Art of Discarding is very straightforward. It's simply a question of becoming conscious of previously unconscious behaviour, and of seeing your approach to possessions as part of the art of living. I hope that the book will help you achieve this.

DON'T SAY IT'S A WASTE

It's very simple: keep things you use and discard those you don't. Things are given life by being used. Keeping something because it would be a waste to get rid of it is a kind of torture. Free yourself from the waste argument, and you'll begin to see the value of things.

THINGS AND THE ENVIRONMENT

Since I originally wrote this book in 2000 environmental awareness has become a key part of society's thinking.

There are now all sorts of regulations about recycling. There are real and online markets for second-hand goods. Environmentally friendly products – from recycled toilet tissue to hybrid cars – are inexpensive and high-quality. We can have environmentally sound lifestyles without thinking about it the whole time.

These are all welcome developments. But has the volume of rubbish reduced? Has stuff stopped accumulating in our homes?

Not as far as I can see. As much rubbish as ever seems to amass. Second-hand shops and markets are overflowing. And, all the while, TV and newspapers churn out endless features on how to use your storage space.

If this awareness were to lead to a general decluttering of lives and homes, then the situation would be different. And the fact that it hasn't done so means, in my view, that there's no real connection between our relationship with things and our awareness of the environment.

ENVIRONMENTAL AWARENESS WON'T SOLVE THE PROBLEM OF TOO MUCH STUFF

It goes without saying that environmental problems have to be thought about on a national or global scale. Issues such as increased entropy or comparative environmental impact feel very distant from our day-to-day existence; it's difficult to maintain both a micro and macro perspective. Even the scientists researching the field can't be certain about the exhaustion of fossil fuels or the growth of holes in the ozone layer. So how are we to take these matters into account in our everyday lives?

At an individual level, environmental awareness can't go much beyond not dropping litter, not pouring milk down the plughole, looking after things and using them carefully, not leaving lights on, reusing shopping bags or buying environmentally sound products.

Let me be clear. I'm not questioning the importance of environmental issues. Society has to develop in a way that takes account of the environment. And, of course, it's better that people know about it than that they are ignorant or uninterested. What I'm saying is, first, that the problems of the environment are too big for individuals alone to deal with, and second, that living environmentally friendly lives is not going to solve the problems that we have with rubbish, the glut of stuff in the world around us or, indeed, in our own homes.

CHANGING HOW WE THINK ABOUT THINGS

Environmental awareness is a valid guideline for life in general. But if we are to solve the specific problem of having too much stuff, we must change the way we deal with it.

For many of us, the thinking has been to bring ever more things into our lives and then keep them all on the basis that it's wasteful to get rid of them. We've assumed that it's good to possess things, and this assumption has encouraged us to have too many.

But possessing things is not good in itself. We have to consider whether they're necessary, whether they're used. And if something's unnecessary, we should get rid of it. This is the essence of the Art of Discarding. Once you appreciate that you don't have to keep what's unnecessary, you'll be better able to use what *is* necessary with proper care.

You don't have to think too much about it. You don't have to resolve at the outset to make do with just a few things. You don't have to tell yourself that treating things with care is good for the environment. Just take each item in turn and ask yourself: is it necessary? Can it be thrown away? This selection process will whittle away at the excess until you reach an optimum level of possession. By then your lifestyle will already be kinder to the environment.

WHEN A SENSE OF WASTE STOPS YOU CLEARING STUFF OUT

I think the Japanese word 'mottainai' (a sense of shame at wastefulness) can be a dangerous one. Its basic meaning suggests damage being done to the essence of something. And to witness such damage gives us pain. It's wonderful that Japanese people think like this and use the word so frequently in their everyday lives (I myself use it when I'm telling my children to eat all their rice), but it can act as a barrier to the question 'Will I actually use this?' It encourages the delusion that just by having something – by not throwing it away – you are doing something positive.

In my opinion the best way to cherish something is to use it. Think about the unwanted gifts that you've put in the cupboard because they're *mottainai*. The food that rots away in the fridge because it's *mottainai*. The pile of department-store carrier bags you've accumulated because they're *mottainai*. Things you've put out for sale on the basis that they're *mottainai*, but which then don't sell and are thrown away by the dealer. It would be a shame if the word *mottainai* came to have no more meaning than this – a mistaken belief that not throwing something away is the same as taking good of care of it.

So don't just store things away for the sake of it. If you value the idea of *mottainai*, think about whether these things are necessary or not. If you can use them, then get on and do so. When they get old, use them for something else. Then, when they've no further potential, dispose of them completely.

This is the kind of *mottainai* that makes sense to me. This is what will allow us to develop a skilful and waste-free approach.

LIVE YOUR OWN LIFE

Have Japanese people always looked after things for as long as they could? You'll hear some people say that there's an old goblin in Japan called Mottainai. It certainly sounds like something that might have figured in an old Japanese tale but, in fact, this goblin was the invention of public-service TV advertising in 1982. A genuine tradition, by contrast, relates to spirits called *Tsukumo-gami*. These were said to enter old, abandoned implements and stir them up to mischief, their message being: 'Don't leave things unused!'

My own feeling is that people in the past were more sensitive when it came to discarding things than we are today. They were sensitive to the souls of things, to their essence (*mottai*), so they felt it was a waste (*mottai-nai*) not to use things that could be used. Then, when they stopped using them, they'd discard them completely and decisively. This is reflected in the *Hari-kuyo* ceremony – a requiem-type service for old needles that is still held at some temples in Japan.

My belief now is the same as it was when I first wrote this book: complete and decisive disposal is of fundamental importance. We have a lot of information available to us these days and we tend to take all of this into account to arrive at solutions. But I feel it is best, as in the past, to think in terms of what is practical and achievable.

As individuals we can only be expected to live in the way our circumstances allow. And there's no reason why we shouldn't try to make things pleasant and easy for ourselves. So you don't have to be thinking about the environment when you buy low-energy products; you may be thinking simply that they save money on electricity. And when you use your own bag for shopping, your reason may just be that it stops you amassing a great pile of supermarket bags.

INTRODUCTION

What do you find difficult to throw away and why?

My urge to tell people to discard things originated one evening when I was with friends who work in publishing. One of them started talking about the trouble she had during an end-of-year clean-up. She couldn't find enough space for all her work-related books and documents. She'd wanted to keep everything for future reference, but her shelves were full. The subject seemed to strike a chord with the others who all confessed to having similar difficulties and described their strategies: 'I put them in a cardboard box,' said one. 'I cut out the articles I wrote and put them in a file,' said another. 'I rent storage space,' said a third. They were laughing about it, but the problem seemed real enough, and it was clear that nobody knew what was best. As I sat chatting with them, I began to wonder: if everyone feels their stuff is such a burden, why don't they just get rid of it? All of their solutions involved storage. Even if they considered filing stuff in a way that reduced the overall volume, none of them went so far as to suggest wholesale disposal.

STUFFED UP

I soon began to realise that this isn't only a problem for my friends and their documents. It's a phenomenon found throughout Japanese society. Economic growth means we've become used to a system of mass production and mass consumption. We've become good at buying things, at choosing things. We're used to thinking carefully about what we want.

And now, in our world of super-abundant supply, something has begun to go wrong.

Take food, for example. Animals on the move are always looking for food: herbivores roam about eating constantly because vegetation has poor nutritional efficiency; carnivores chase their prey, and when they catch it they eat their fill, then sleep until they are hungry again. In the natural world, hunger is normal, and animals' bodies have a system for responding to it.

But humans have more food than is necessary. Surrounded by all this food, we have to control what we eat, manage our intake. Hunger is a vital, basic mechanism to which the human body responds, but there's no signal when we eat too much. If something looks delicious, we eat; when it's mealtime, we eat. There's no end to it.

And the situation with things is similar. Just as we should not accept too much food, so we should not allow too many things to accumulate around us. Food may be delicious and nutritious, but there has to be a limit; things may be cheap, good quality and useful, but we can't go on piling them up. Yet our senses have no signal to tell us we have too much.

If you take a step back and look at the way we're surrounded by things, doesn't it seem unnatural, irrational?

HAVING THINGS IS HUMAN NATURE

Where does our desire to have things come from?

The answer's easy for food. Along with sex and sleep, eating is one of the acts from which individuals derive basic happiness and fulfilment. But our desire to possess objects other than food seems to me to be bound up with our sense of existence.

Things are not simply physical objects. Once we possess them they become part of us. This is the fundamental logic of the consumer society – the feeling that self-realisation is achieved through having the things we want. And if we lose something we've obtained, we feel pain at losing part of the self we've built up. When a toddler develops signs of ego, he wants to monopolise his toys and won't let other children touch them. It's only later, when he develops an awareness of others that he is able to share with friends or his little brother.

I think the toddler's impulse remains with us in adulthood, albeit concealed beneath a veneer of rationality. It makes us hoard things that we obtain, and when we get rid of something it makes us buy something better to replace it. This seems to be natural behaviour.

Yet at the same time, everyone seems somehow to feel

that our glut of possessions is very *un*natural – a sense of unease that manifests itself in an interest in environmental problems and economical lifestyles.

While cutting waste and minimising consumption are good things – kind to the planet and to household finances, I don't feel that such a complete change of direction is possible for society as a whole.

I think we should accept the fact of possessions and people's desire to have them. It's part of human nature. We can't change it and it won't change of its own accord. What should be changed, though, is the tendency to carry on possessing things without being aware of what we're doing.

THE IDEA OF 'DISCARDING'

We must stop simply having stuff and putting it away some-where. We need to think more actively about our relationship with things. This means a major change in attitude, enabling us to engage with the idea of discarding, and to develop the skills that will help us to do it.

The task of discarding isn't just a question of chucking things in the rubbish. Like the publishing friends I mentioned earlier, people often worry about it. But if, in spite of such uncertainties, you can be selective in what you keep, you'll develop an idea of how much stuff is enough for you to live with. Then, once you have rid yourself of the excess, economical and environ-mentally friendly lifestyles (buying the bare minimum, recycling, etc.) can become useful methods of managing possessions.

Having read this far you might now be inspired to think, OK, let's get rid of this stuff! But where to start? How do you get rid of all the stuff you've accumulated? You may well throw your hands up in despair and give up before you've even started.

To deter you from giving up, I'll now talk a bit about my own experience. Then I'll introduce a survey I conducted. Using examples from that survey, I'll move on in the following parts to specific attitudes to and strategies for disposal.

MOVING HOUSE AND THE IMPORTANCE OF DISPOSAL

It was moving house that made me realise the importance of getting rid of things. At twenty-six I moved out of my parents' house to a small one-room flat with a lavatory, but no bath. From there I went to a two-bedroom flat, then a two-bedroom house. Three moves in three years. Then I married and moved again. At first we rented a three-bedroom house and a separate small flat for work, but then a few years later we bought a bigger house. All told, I moved five times in eight years.

Awareness dawned during that first move to the independence of a small flat. With my limited funds I arranged a small truck and, wanting to take the bare minimum, I began sorting through my possessions. As I decided what to take, I was surprised to find that many of the books, mementos, and even furniture that had seemed so important to me would be unnecessary in my new place.

My new flat felt good with just the essentials in it. But the volume of stuff in my parents' house seemed almost the same as before – I'd left there all the things that I could have got rid of.

Inevitably, after each subsequent move to larger accommodation the amount of stuff around me grew. But by then I knew the importance of disposal and I never kept too much as I moved from place to place.

MARRIAGE AND THE PLEASURE OF DISPOSAL

Marriage brought a new problem. My husband had lived for almost ten years in the three-bedroom house we now shared. It was built in the early-twentieth-century Taisho Period, and was a generous size. It had plenty of storage and was full of nooks and crannies one hardly even noticed.

Naturally enough, a lot of stuff had accumulated: light fittings and flowerpots that might come in handy one day; vases and chests that had been placed here and there 'for the time being'; the contents of said chests – bags, plates, cups, bowls . . .

None of this was rubbish. All of it could be useful. But with another person coming to live there, available space inevitably shrank and things started to get in the way. And that other person was me – someone who had become aware of the potential for discarding.

Naturally, I began to get rid of things. Looked at with an eye to disposal, it was surprising how almost everything seemed a suitable target. And since it was all stuff that had been accumulated by someone else, it seemed easy to decide. But my spouse resisted: 'I want this' . . . 'You can't get rid of that' . . . 'Don't touch the books' and so on. I then had to persuade him how important it is to get rid of things – that while it is wasteful in one sense, this is outweighed by the value of securing more space.

In the end, when hostilities were over, my spouse stopped complaining and began to be happy with how neat and tidy the place was becoming. And his happiness made me all the more happy myself.

This experience made the idea of discarding even more significant than it had been before. I began to feel a sense of joy at seeing a place cleared of clutter. My mind was filled with phrases I'd heard about the beauty of use and function-ality. I thought of the Katsura Imperial Villa in Kyoto, famous for its simplicity.

At the end of the process, our home was a very pleasant place – one that others envied. And while there may have been one or two things that I regretted getting rid of, I have no recollection of that now.

Nevertheless, when we moved on to our current house there were still piles of large items to be thrown away. It was enough to make me despair. Even after we'd left, I had to return to the old, empty house day after day to put out more rubbish. I gazed at the piles, disgusted at the idea that irre-spective of our belief in getting rid of things, we'd still been living with so much unnecessary stuff.

Is the situation any different at your house?

CONFLICT WITH MY POST-WAR-THINKING
MOTHER

Another big factor behind my belief in disposal is my mother.

My mother belongs to the generation that grew up during and after the Second World War. She married soon after leaving school and for the next fifteen years lived in a large house with an outside storage shed. She then moved to a flat, where she has been living for twenty years.

I recall my childhood home as a space that was constantly under the occupation of things. And even since her two children left and got married, the number of things in my mother's home hasn't decreased. On the contrary, there seem to be more now than ever.

Take the tableware cupboard, for example. It's jam-packed. There are remnants of the Western set my parents bought just after they were married, one cup from a Japanese tea set, a little pot received at a wedding, a glass obtained in a shop promotion, a lacquer bowl I'd given my mother . . . Even though she's living alone, she has three times as much tableware as we have.

If I suggest that she gets rid of some of it, she'll say, 'I know. I really should,' but doesn't. If I suggest doing it for her, she says she'll do it herself. And I understand why she feels she can't. As children in the post-war years her generation knew real want. They were marrying at a time when the country had begun to produce a succession of new home-electrical and other products. Things are precious to them. They can't throw away something useable without a sense of guilt.

Old towels and chipped teacups – objects that other people would have thrown out long ago – are, for my mother, things that should still be put to use. There is certainly virtue in feeling this way. But unfortunately it's a virtue that doesn't count for much now, when new things come along well before older things have reached the end of their useful lives.

I hope that the message of this book will reach people of my mother's generation, people who share those same virtues and values. They must start to discard things, and come to see this as a virtue too.

SO WHAT ABOUT THE ROOM I WORK IN?

I expect you now think that I live a highly efficient, clutter-free life, surrounded only by the most carefully selected objects.

Well, not quite. I keep getting rid of stuff, but it keeps on accumulating. I suppose that overall my home has less stuff in it than most others. But things proliferate in no time, slipping in through the narrowest gaps.

Let's take a look at the room where I'm writing now.

On and around the desk:

- A pen holder with too much in it: some of the pens have been there for years and no longer work at all; there's a nicely designed paper knife that looks rather important, but I know I'm never going to use it; a little Miffy toy someone gave me has been hanging there for months.

- A pile of floppy disks: since I now exchange data by email and store major items on an MO drive, I don't use floppy disks. I don't even know what's been stored on the disks in the pile – bad organisation means the labels haven't been filled in.
- Desk drawers: I've emptied them out and sorted through the contents every time I've moved, but still they're full of old notebooks and documents. They're not functioning as drawers. I only open them once a month at most.

On the floor:

- A bamboo foot massager someone gave me is lying under the chair, always getting in the way.
- Piles of faxes, photocopies and magazines have merged into a single mound. At the bottom somewhere must be the remnants of last month's work.
- Piles of books: one comprises some that aren't worth keeping and others I've borrowed from the library; another, belonging to my husband, has been sitting next to the bookcase for two years, ever since we moved. I knock into it sometimes and it collapses, but I just stack the books up again.

On the wall:

- A summer coat that wouldn't fit in the cupboard has been hanging on the wall since last autumn.

In the cupboard:

• Paperbacks and the vacuum cleaner are neatly stored at the bottom, but the top is full of clothes I never wear and bags I never use.

I'll stop there. If I describe any more, I'll begin to feel ill! But bear in mind that I dispose of at least one large bag of burnable rubbish every week. If I didn't, the situation would be far worse.

THE 'CAN'T-DISCARD' SURVEY

That's enough about my personal experience. Now let's take a look at what other people feel they can't get rid of.

I conducted what I call the 'Can't-discard' survey – an informal investigation of the items in everyday life that caused people problems in terms of storage, tidying up or disposal, based on my publisher's editing department and my own circle of acquaintances. This means the sample is mainly urban, white-collar, but there is no other specific bias in terms of lifestyle, income or job. The majority of responses were from the Tokyo area, but some were also from Osaka, Kyushu, Shikoku, Chubu and Hokuriku. Although the data-collection methods and number of partici-pants mean that the results are not valid statistically, it does give a good picture of the attitudes of contemporary city dwellers.

Respondents were asked:

- Are there any things in your everyday life you find difficult to store?
- Are there any things or places that always seem untidy?
- When you see a particular thing or look in a particular place, do you always feel you should do something about it?

Almost all respondents (100 per cent of men and 98 per cent of women) answered 'Yes' to these questions. This high 'Yes' response rate was expected. It seemed to me that people were almost bound to have this kind of problem. In fact, I found it remarkable that anyone at all said 'No'.

When asked what particular types of thing caused difficulties, in terms of what to do with them, it became clear that the top three problem areas were books, clothes and magazines. For men, books were first and clothes second. For women, clothes first, books second. Magazines were in third position for both genders. Although I expected people to have problems with these items, I was surprised to find that books and clothes caused difficulties for about half of both gender groups.

The next question helped clarify their psychology:

- Are there things you feel you should discard, but can't bring yourself to?

Eighty per cent of men and 95 per cent of women said 'Yes'. Looked at from the opposite angle, this means that just over 10 per cent of the overall sample couldn't think of any items to classify in this way. This contrasts with the response to the previous question, to which almost everybody responded that there were things they didn't know what to do with. Thus, it seems that some people don't know what to do with things, but never consider discarding them.

For men, books topped the list of things that they felt uncomfortable getting rid of. This was followed by magazines and clothes. For women, it was clothes, followed by books and then photographs. The items that people feel uncomfortable getting rid of overlap substantially with those they don't know what to do with. As I expected, there was a bias towards information-related items for men and clothes for women.

If you don't know what to do with something, disposal is an option

In this book I want to suggest that you keep the option of disposal in mind – 'Don't know what to do with it = think about discarding it'.

When the decision to discard something is not that difficult, everybody does it. If you don't like the idea, consider the survey results. Respondents identified things they made a point of getting rid of to avoid accumulation. Top of the list were magazines (third on the list of items that people didn't know what to do with) – 40 per cent of men and 60 per cent of women get rid of magazines quickly to avoid them building up.

Perhaps for women, the limited content of fashion and information magazines makes them comparatively easy to throw away (they rank only fifth in the list of things women found tough to dispose of).

Other things that people make a point of discarding include advertising and mailshots, supermarket and department-store carrier bags, pamphlets, catalogues and newspapers. It is easy to decide that these things are no longer necessary, although a more powerful factor behind their disposal is the fear of accumulation. Knowing this fear is the discarder's first step.

Things that cause problems

Having taken a quick look at the results of the survey, I'd like to go back and look in detail at some of the examples respondents gave.

As I've said already, the items that people most often have difficulty dealing with are books, magazines and clothes. If we consider these, together with the many other examples that respondents gave, some overall patterns start to become clear:

1. Things with high information content – books, magazines, documents (including work documents), pamphlets and

catalogues. People find it hard to get rid of these because they worry there'll be a problem later – that they'll become necessary at some stage. But the volume of such items just keeps increasing. What's more, if you don't have a good indexing system, you won't be able to use them efficiently in any case, so a lot of effort has to go into storing them.

2. Clothes, shoes, bags etc. Because these are things that are worn or carried, people tend to grow fond of them. They don't have a use-by date and they often last a very long time. One reason they can cause difficulties is a shortage of storage space. The problem becomes clear once your cupboard is full.

3. Leisure items such as videos and CDs. People like to keep these because they want ready access to particular films or music. But they're difficult to store in a way that makes access easy. In this respect, they're psychologically similar to objects in point 1, above.

4. Things with special emotional significance. There are a lot of these – not just obvious things like photos, presents and birthday cards, but also, for example, clothes your mother made, toys the children no longer use, a television you bought when you were first married or reference books you used when you were a student can be hard to dispose of, not so much for their information content as for the memories of your years of study.

5. Things it seems a waste to get rid of. Food is a typical example. It seems wrong to throw it away. Getting rid of expensive things also seems wasteful, for example branded

shoes or designer clothing. People feel such things should be looked after. Books and presents can also can be classified in this way.

The hidden psychology of 'discarding'

Survey respondents were asked to choose possible solutions from a prepared list for items they didn't know what to do with. The most popular choice for both men and women was 'discard'. The nature of the survey may have encouraged participants towards this response, but even so, they certainly seemed to feel that such things should be discarded if possible.

The second choice for women (selected by almost half) was solving the problem by developing better storage and organisation skills. Perhaps this reflects the power of social assumptions about women and tidiness.

A lot of men, on the other hand, would like to solve the problem by moving to a bigger home. One can almost hear them sighing: 'If only there was more room!' I understand how they feel, but it seems rather optimistic to suppose that a bigger place would look tidier. Women may think about expanding storage space, but they don't appear to believe that a bigger house would solve the problem. This seems to be a difference between men and women.

In the survey, I asked people for associations with the Japanese word 'suteru' (meaning discard, get rid of). This also revealed interesting psychological patterns. On the one hand there were associations like 'feels good', 'decisive', 'new start', 'fresh', 'light', 'moving house', 'minimalist', 'simple life'. This must reflect the mindset of people who chose 'discard' as the best solution to their clutter problems. On the other hand, there were associations such as, 'It may be necessary one day', 'I might regret it', and 'organisation'. Presumably, these people's preferred solutions were better storage and organisation methods. The unease reflected in these associations links to others such as 'memory', 'attachment', 'goodbye', 'parting', 'woman', 'man', 'past', 'go', 'abandoning parents' and 'disappear'. I was surprised that a number of people mentioned an association with the historical practice of abandoning old people in the mountains. It is clearly a deep-rooted image.

I suppose it was natural that while many people thought of expressions that associate very directly with 'discard' – 'rubbish', 'rubbish bag', 'land-fill' – many others gave expressions that suggested ecological concerns: 'waste', 'dioxins' 'recycle', 'flea market', 'processing plant', 'pollute the world', 'perhaps someone could take it'.

BE BRAVE – GET RID OF THINGS

I hope that from the results of the survey you will have realised that while discarding seems simple enough at first glance, it does, in fact, involve quite complex psychology.

This is apparent in the word-association exercise above. Here, individuals often saw the act of 'discarding' from different angles at the same time. For example, one said 'a waste', but also 'feels good' and 'decisive'. Another said 'recycle' at the same time as 'past' and 'light'.

Sometimes, rather than struggle with this psychology it can seem easier to let things pile up. But that's a delusion. Don't be a dormouse, hiding in a hole in a tree among your leaves and nuts. Letting stuff pile up will only cause trouble in the end. Be brave and get rid of it.

PART ONE

You can master the art of discarding

Ten attitudes to help you get rid of things

1

DON'T KEEP IT 'FOR NOW'

People who accumulate things are fond of saying 'let's just keep it for now' or 'we'll hang on to it for the time being'. But nothing's going to change, so there's no point in putting off the decision.

Danger items

People will keep anything 'for now', from information items (documents, magazines, flyers, mailshots, etc.) to food, clothes, gifts, furniture and appliances.

When does it happen?

Hanging on to something 'for now' is an easy way out, so we tend to do so in lots of different situations. Here are some examples:

SITUATION 1: READING THE NEWSPAPER IN THE MORNING

Full of flyers as usual. Mm . . . could be some useful

information in this lot. Hey, this stuff looks cheap . . . I want a new computer. Ah, a sale at that posh department store . . . That reminds me – I haven't got enough shirts for the warm weather. Well, I'm too busy to look at these now, but I can read them this evening when I get home. The wife's not got a lot to do, so I dare say she'll read through them all this morning. She'd better not throw them away. 'Keep this lot for now, dear, till I can have a look at them.'

SITUATION 2: BACK FROM SHOPPING – YOU WANT TO PUT THINGS IN THE FRIDGE

What's all this? How am I going to get my shopping in there? Well, I'm going to use it this evening anyway, so I suppose I'll try to slip it in at the front. Oh dear, those jars at the back – where did they come from? I'll have to sort all this stuff out. But I'll leave it for now. Oh no! There's no space for the natto! Perhaps it'll squeeze into the vegetable compartment. Oh, look at that wilting spinach! Well, I've already decided what to have today . . . maybe we can have it tomorrow. I'll keep it for the time being.

SITUATION 3: YOU GET A DELIVERY

A summer gift from Mrs Tatsumi . . . Oh dear! More dried noodles! Never mind! Well, we won't use them straight away, so I'll put them in the cupboard. Ugh, the box won't fit! Oh well, I can get rid of some of this packaging. Yes, that'll do. Good, I'll keep them for the time being.

SITUATION 4: BACK FROM A WEDDING

The couple has gone to the trouble of choosing individual presents for each of the guests . . . What have they given me? Well, that's a surprise. Not quite my kind of thing. Can't be helped. They'll notice if they come round and it's not on display. I'd better hang on to it for the time being.

SITUATION 5: YOU'VE BOUGHT A NEW LAMP

Yes, it's a great design. Perfect for the room. Now, what shall we do with the rattan shade we've always had? It would be a waste to throw it out. It's still in good shape. I like the design too in a way. Let's keep it for now and maybe we'll find a use for it.

SITUATION 6: YOU'VE JUST FINISHED A
BUSINESS MEETING

That was a surprise! I never thought they'd send that many people. I was lucky to have enough business cards. But what about all the cards they gave me? I can't even remember who was who. But I may as well keep them for the time being. And then there are all these documents . . . The contract's gone through so it's not my responsibility now – I won't really be involved. But, I suppose I'd better keep the documents for now, just in case.

The 'keep-for-now' mentality

I'm sure the situations above will be familiar to many readers. Let's consider whether the characters involved have anything to gain from 'keeping things for now'.

In Situation 1 we can imagine the flyers piled up on the dining table. When the husband comes home late from the office he's going to be much more interested in having a bath and watching TV. His wife will say, 'Are you going to read these?' and he'll say, 'Of course! I said I would, didn't I?' He'll then give them a quick glance, and that will be the end of it.

In Situation 2 the woman will take the jars out of the fridge some time later and be horrified to find the contents mouldy. The spinach will wilt away in the vegetable compartment for another week, before finally being thrown out.

Situation 3 will be resolved in the end-of-year clean-up. 'What's this?' they'll say, as they look in the cupboard. Then they'll open the packaging to find the noodles rendered inedible by humidity.

The newlyweds in Situation 4 will never come round and their present will end up being put away somewhere. The old light shade in Situation 5 is destined to occupy the corner of a cupboard for years before finally being thrown away when the owners move, and the business cards in Situation 6 will just fill up the person's card holder, making it irritatingly bulky, while the documents will lie at the back of a drawer, their purpose entirely forgotten.

The truth is that most of these items have been a nuisance from the moment they were received or replaced. They could have been thrown away immediately, but people don't face up to that. They keep the item in question 'for now', only to persuade themselves sometime in the future that it should go: 'Well, we kept it, but we didn't use it, so . . .'

Slightly damaged items are often treated this way too – a teacup with a fine crack, a pen that doesn't write very well, a blouse with a small stain . . . These are nuisance items as well, but it somehow seems a waste to get rid of them, so we hang on to them 'for the time being'.

Things that are kept 'for now' are in a kind of limbo, held back on the brink of becoming rubbish. 'For the time being', 'for now' are just ways of escaping the act of disposal.

When something is actually necessary, the 'for now' psychology does not come into play at all.

In a way the 'keep-for-now' response is like the Recycle bin on a computer. If you send a document to the Recycle bin it's no longer in front of you. But it hasn't really disappeared. It's still on the hard drive. It's only when you 'empty your bin' that you really get rid of the document and it's deleted from your hard drive.

But there's one big difference between a computer and the real world. A computer's Recycle bin can fill up without using any physical space, and if you exceed capacity old files are automatically deleted. But in the real world, if you put something somewhere 'for now' it will occupy that space until you finally get rid of it.

Think like this!

Don't let the 'for now' idea even enter your head. If you really want to look at a flyer, pick it up straight away. If you're bothered by jars in the fridge, take them out immediately. If you receive a gift of food, take it out of its box and place it somewhere where it stands a chance of being eaten. Even if you're unlikely to consume it now, take it out of the box anyway. The fancier the box, the more likely people are to leave the food inside, but if you take it out you'll find you get an opportunity to eat it and share it.

People often feel it's a waste to throw away lamps, appliances or furniture, so they end up keeping them 'for the time being'. But you must find another way out. Use second-hand shops or your network of friends. I'll talk more about these later.

Documents, business cards and magazines can be very difficult to deal with, but again, don't just keep them 'for now'.

The function of a business card is that it helps when you want to make contact with someone. There's no point having the cards of lots of different people from the same department of the same company. And unless the name on the card means something to you, the chances of you ever having to contact the person in question are very slim. When you put documents or magazines away somewhere, ask yourself what exactly you want to keep them for. If you keep them for no particular reason, they'll just get in the way and make it more difficult to find things that are genuinely important. If you're going to keep them, have a clear reason for doing so. (I'll say more about papers and documents under Attitude 7.)

2

AVOID 'TEMPORARY' STORAGE – DECIDE NOW!

Things we decide to hang on to 'for now' tend to have no clear potential use. Where we have a specific function in mind there's a danger of allotting things a 'temporary' or 'provisional' home. And the problem then is that 'temporary' often ends up permanent.

Danger items

Anything that we feel should be retained and organised – books, CDs, videos, documents; things that are stored, but at the same time used regularly – food, clothes; stationery and other everyday items.

When does it happen?

It may be simplest to take some examples from the workplace.

Imagine a desk. You've allocated the side drawers as follows: top drawer – stationery; second drawer – PC equipment; bottom drawer – documents for retention. The wide drawer above your knees is for notebooks and work in progress.

But things defy this classification and start encroaching into areas they shouldn't.

SITUATION 1: ON TOP OF YOUR DESK

On your desk there's a pile of stuff you regard as current: documents relating to a plan in progress; journals you have to read; a weekly news magazine you bought yesterday. You've put them there together 'temporarily'. You've just finished a meeting and decide to put the papers from that on the same pile – you may want them next week, so you think they might as well go there temporarily too. If you were to put them away, you might forget where you've put them.

SITUATION 2: YOU'VE COMPLETED A PROJECT

Recently, you've been working on a plan. You've done similar work in the past and so you took papers out of the old file and kept them on your project desk. Now it's complete and responsibility is passing to someone else, so you think you'll get rid of unnecessary papers. But the current documents are mixed up with old ones. If you throw the old report away, there'll be no copy left. You don't have time to sort through every single piece of paper, so as a 'temporary' measure you put everything together in the old file.

SITUATION 3: SOMETHING INTERRUPTS YOUR FLOW

You've just printed out some presentation documents when something more urgent comes up. You slip the documents into a drawer 'temporarily'. They're not worth filing away yet, and you're about to copy them anyway. Besides, you've kept them on the computer.

SITUATION 4: MISCELLANEOUS!

You have a lot of stuff that doesn't fit neatly into your drawers' allocations: a guarantee, a catalogue, some photographs, some biscuits somebody gave you, a lighter, etc. You're not sure where to put them, but there's some space in the wide drawer above your knees so you shove them in there.

SITUATION 5: PAPERWORK IS MOUNTING

The number of documents you have to keep is increasing fast, so you decide to store them 'temporarily' in a cardboard box at your feet. You can just drop everything in there. It makes life easy. The box has plenty of capacity. You'll get around to sorting the documents out properly in due course.

The 'temporary' mentality

You may intend to put something in a place 'temporarily', but once it's there, the chances are you'll never move it. Even if the place is unsuitable, it's very unlikely you'll change it. If there's a box in a corridor, people tend to just walk past it – nobody thinks to move it. If there's a pile of papers occupying your limited desk space, you'll probably just push it to one side. It's a pain to do anything else. The number of 'temporary' items grows and the situation gets out of control. Here are some of the things that happen:

i.   You forget they exist (Situation 1).
ii.   You don't know where you've put them (Situations 3, 4).
iii. You put them away and you never see them again (Situations 2, 4, 5).
iv.   Important things get mixed up with unimportant things (Situations 1, 2, 5).
v.   You keep putting things in the same place because it's easy (Situations 1, 2, 5).

You obviously won't be able to take advantage of things if you've forgotten they exist (i). If you can't remember where they are, you won't be able to find them (ii). If you store them away without much thought, you probably won't use them again (iii). If you've mixed necessary and unnecessary things together, it will be difficult to move items or throw items away (iv). If you start putting things in a particular place because it's easy to do so, that place will end up as a kind of rubbish dump (v).

Of course, this doesn't just happen in the workplace – it happens at home too: in living rooms, kitchens, bedrooms.

In fact, there are very few things that don't get this 'temporary' treatment. Keeping things 'for now' or putting them some-where 'temporarily' is very natural human behaviour.

It reminds me of squirrels in the forest. They bury nuts as stock, but sometimes forget about them. When spring comes the forgotten nuts germinate and saplings start to grow. It's a kind of co-operative relationship between squirrels and trees, based on food and reproduction. But is there any benefit in our own tendency to store things 'temporarily'?

Think like this!

When we're surrounded by so much stuff, this kind of care-less 'temporary' storage is just dangerous. It makes it more difficult both to get rid of things, and to find important things when necessary.

We have to be firm – make decisions now. If you feel like putting documents on the top of a pile, stop. If you're about to put some tins of soup in the tableware cupboard, stop. If you've been given a freebie hand towel, don't just shove it into an empty space in the wardrobe. Think: 'Is this really the place for it?'

Half the documents can probably be thrown away; the rest can be put in a file. If you're thinking of putting tins of soup in the tableware cupboard, then your shelf for tins must be full. Some of the tins already there are probably out of date. Or perhaps space is taken up with old *bento* boxes or packs of tissues. As for the hand towel, why not put it straight in the boot of the car as a cleaning cloth? Or if you've got plenty of car cloths already, you could use it to wipe the floor and throw it away.

You'll often find that avoiding 'temporary' storage for one thing will reveal other things that should be thrown away.

(3)

'SOMETIME' NEVER COMES

You can say things like 'I may use it sometime', or, 'One day it may be useful' until the cows come home. Little girls dream that some day a prince will come along – but that day is never likely to arrive. And before she knows it, the little girl is a middle-aged woman . . .

Danger items

Clothes, bags and accessories; books, magazines, documents, pamphlets, catalogues; videos and negatives; presents; light fixtures and televisions, etc. that are being replaced.

When does it happen?

'Sometime' often crops up when people aren't sure whether to get rid of something. You don't have a clear basis for decision making, so you use 'sometime' as an escape route.

SITUATION 1: PUTTING CLOTHES IN THE WARDROBE

The wardrobe's so full everything's getting creased. I'd better sort it out. Now, what's this? Something I haven't worn for a while! It looks rather small – I'm getting a bit fat round the middle. But I liked it when I bought it, and I may lose weight sometime. Yes, I think I'll keep it. What about this? I suppose I should get rid of it – I got it when I was a student. The design's really old. But then 1970s clothes are getting popular again. I may want to wear it sometime.

SITUATION 2: LOOKING AT AN INTERIORS CATALOGUE

I'm so glad we changed the curtains. This is a really useful catalogue. Look at these lights, and the basin. Very smart. Beautiful interiors. We may want to get new furniture sometime. I'll keep the catalogue for reference.

SITUATION 3: TIDYING UP A PHOTO ALBUM

Children grow so fast! All these photographs . . . When she was a baby we took five rolls of film every month. Oh dear! The negatives box is completely full. Perhaps I'd better throw some old ones away. But what if she wants her own copies when she's grown up? I'd better not get rid of them, after all. They may be useful sometime.

SITUATION 4: BACK FROM A WEDDING

That was a grand affair! Look at this huge thank-you present bag – that's Nagoya for you! I wonder what's inside. A great big box. Wait a moment . . . a zaru soba set. It looks expensive. But I can't remember us ever eating zaru soba. I wonder if we'll use it. But it seems a shame to give it away. We might use it sometime, so let's hang on to it.

SITUATION 5: BACK FROM THE ELECTRICAL STORE

Here we are – a thirty-six-inch TV! Makes the twenty-four-inch one look small, doesn't it? It's certainly the bigger the better when it comes to a television. Now what about the old one? There's nowhere for it to go. We've already got one in our bedroom, and the children have got one too. Shall we get rid of it? But it costs five hundred yen to have something that size taken away. And it still works perfectly. Someone might want it sometime. Let's put it away till then.

SITUATION 6: OPENING A DELIVERY

Mum's sent some miso. Wonderful! It's come in a special parcel box. Typical of her. She really likes to do things properly. What shall we do with the box? It's in good condition. It might be useful when we send something ourselves. Or if we move house . . . it's always difficult trying to collect cardboard boxes for a move. I'll keep it. I expect we'll use it sometime.

The 'sometime' or 'one day' mentality

Our survey showed that above all it was books, magazines and clothes that people have difficulty dealing with parting with. It's a problem caused by the 'sometime' mentality, which generally applies to things that can still be used, rather than things like rotten food or broken TVs.

The character in Situation 1 is middle-aged; his shape won't change until he's far too old to wear a young person's clothes. And even if fashion comes full circle, the clothes are still going to look old and he'll never wear them.

The person in Situation 2 may buy new light fixtures or furniture in years to come; but if and when they do they'll want to look at the latest catalogues, not the one they have now.

The negatives in Situation 3 will just accumulate, and no one will ever use them to make new prints. The soba set in Situation 4 will never be used. No one will ever want the old TV in Situation 5 and the people concerned will eventually pay for it to be taken away. And boxes like the one in Situation 6 simply accumulate, taking up space at the top of a cupboard.

Let's take the example of clothes. All of us have had the experience of opening a wardrobe, seeing something that looks rather good and thinking, Yes, now's my chance to wear it – *sometime* has come! But then we put it on and realise it's not quite right. There's always a reason why we stop wearing something, or why we never wore it in the first place. But we don't think through these reasons carefully. We just see that things *look* wearable and keep them. That's how they accumulate.

Ultimately, the 'sometime' mentality is another version of the 'waste' mentality. You don't want to dispose of something because it's a waste. If you keep it, you feel there'll be a chance to use it 'sometime'. But you have no idea when that might be. If you do have a definite idea of when, then you have a clear reason for keeping it – the vague notion of 'sometime' doesn't cross your mind.

Think like this!

The best way to tackle the 'sometime' or 'I'll use it one day' mentality is to tell yourself: 'No use in three years means no use at all.' A period of three years can be applied to almost all day-to-day items – clothes, plates, TVs, fans, futons, telephones, back-issue magazines, empty boxes, etc. If you have had the opportunity to use the item during those three years, but didn't, just face the fact that it's not necessary – before three years turn into thirty.

Of course, three years is not appropriate for everything. Meeting documents or magazines, for example, have a shorter cycle, so set different periods for them, as applicable – maybe three months or a year. And for some items a longer period may be necessary. The essential thing is to adopt the attitude that if you haven't used something for a certain period, you're never going to.

(And at the risk of going on too much about the girl and her prince mentioned earlier, I'd suggest that if he doesn't arrive in three years, she'd better settle down with an old childhood playmate before she gets too old.)

4

'REALLY CONVENIENT!' TO SOMEBODY
ELSE – IRRITATING JUNK TO ME

A re you living a really inconvenient life surrounded by 'really convenient' devices? If you can break the spell of 'convenience', you'll see how the illusory value of things just falls away.

Danger items

This is an issue particularly with gadgets, tools and appliances, but can also apply to other things you obtain in case of a particular eventuality.

When does it happen?

Tools and appliances have particular functions: scissors cut, pots are for boiling, screwdrivers are for turning screws . . . With such clear uses, why would you want to get rid of them? Well, the danger lies right there – in their supposedly convenient functions.

SITUATION 1: A JUICER YOU BUY AT A DEPARTMENT-STORE DEMONSTRATION

My husband's always eating out, so he never has enough vegetables. Juicers have a bad press though, don't they? People buy them and don't use them. But this one's different? The old ones were difficult to clean, but this one's easy? I see. You just take this out? Well, it looks good. Convenient. I'll have one – for the sake of my husband's health.

SITUATION 2: A FRIEND HAS GIVEN YOU A SLOW COOKER

It cooks on its own, wonderful for stews. But I can't really think how I'm going to use it. It saves on gas and it's safe, so that's good. My friend used it for a year and said it was really convenient. She doesn't exaggerate, and her cooking's about the same level as mine. If she says it's useful, then it must be. Maybe I'll use it when the baby's older and eats more. I'll keep it a bit longer.

SITUATION 3: YOU SEE A NEIGHBOUR USING LONG-HANDLED PRUNERS

I don't feel safe on this step ladder cutting these branches. The wife won't help at all. Oh! The woman next door's using something interesting. Looks good. Very quick. I'll have a word with her. Long-handled pruners? Easy for women to use, you say? Really convenient? I see. We'll try some. What? We've got some already? The wife bought some at the same time as you did? I didn't know that. She's always said she couldn't reach the branches.

SITUATION 4: SOFTWARE YOU WERE TOLD ABOUT BY A COLLEAGUE

I've had a PC for about a year now and I feel I can just about use it for work. But I have more and more files and I keep losing track of where they are. I'm doing lots of different types of work now – maybe I'd better use that management software my colleague installed for me. Apparently, it sorts files automatically by name and date, and it's got a good a search function. He said it was really good for people who use PCs for work. He persuaded me to have it. But I'm not sure about it. Can someone like me handle it? Maybe I could . . . once I'm more used to the PC. I suppose my colleague must be right. He knows all about computers. I'll leave it installed for a while.

SITUATION 5: INSTANT MEALS RECOMMENDED BY A FRIEND

It's such a pain cooking when you come home late. That's the problem with living alone. I'm going to stock up with those long-life ready meals Yuko recommended. They last a long time, so I won't have to eat them all quickly. And when you want one, it's only a question of heating it up. Yuko said they're really convenient. Let's have a look at the label. Yes, they keep for a while. Oh, I think I'll buy ten.

SITUATION 6: A COLD COMPRESS USED AT NURSERY SCHOOL

So this is the cold compress advertised on TV? My daughter's always getting a temperature, so it could be useful. The child in the adverts seems very happy sleeping with one on his forehead. I'll try one on Saya. I'll ask the teacher which brand is best. They're all the same, she says. It's a really good idea to get a pack for the first-aid box, she says. Well, she works with children, so I'll take her advice.

The 'really useful' mentality

One only has to think of the constant profitability of pyramid sales schemes to see how enticing 'convenience' can be. But you can see how the situations described above will pan out. The software in Situation 4 will remain a mystery, staying unused, taking up space on the hard disk. The person in Situation 5 will carry on eating out or grabbing pot noodles at a convenience store on the way home; microwave meals are not a part of her life, and by the time she remembers them, they'll be past their use-by date . . .

Of course, most of the recommendations that we encounter in daily life come with the best of intentions, a factor which only makes things worse. People who've found something useful can be very persuasive, and when they say it will be 'great for *you*' it's very hard not to be persuaded.

Let me put this in a wider context. It seems to me that Japanese people in the decades after the war were swept up with this idea of 'convenience'. Rice-cooker jars from electricity companies, twenty-four hour baths from gas companies, sticky-tape cutters from stationery companies, new models from motor companies – all marketed on the basis of 'convenience'. The message was never a gentle 'It's really convenient, so why don't you try it? It was more a question of 'It's REALLY CONVENIENT so you've GOT TO use it!'

If you consider post-war history, it's not surprising that a lot of housewives suffer from a kind of 'really convenient' syndrome. I mentioned my mother's generation in the introduction – they were particularly vulnerable. And it was infectious. *A* would recommend something to *B* and then *B* would recommend it to *C* and so on. (I can't count the number of things I have that my mother has recommended as 'convenient'!)

Another set of people who are particularly vulnerable to the 'real convenience' syndrome are those who are entering a new stage of life. There's the 'really useful' business-card holder they get from an uncle when they start work, the flood of 'really useful' gifts they receive when they first have children, the 'really useful' pots and appliances a daughter gets from her mother when she moves away from home for the first time. They'll give them a go and try their best to appreciate their convenience. But it doesn't take long to find out that these extremely convenient items are nothing of the sort. They just get in the way.

Of course, having said all that, some things you get really are really useful. Just pick wisely.

Think like this!

The key is to know yourself.

You're not someone else. You're you. If you keep this in mind, then you'll know that you don't want things that don't seem necessary. After the war every time a company developed a product it tried to create a demand for it. Their products didn't develop in response to existing 'needs'; the 'needs' were generated for the product. I won't go into a detailed discussion of marketing here, but what I will say is that it's about time we were free from that kind of strategy.

$$5$$

NOTHING IS SACRED

'Sacred' is a status given to certain things irrespective of usefulness or age. It has little to do with their true value.

Danger items

Documents, mementos, food, books, etc.

When does it happen?

The following situations show typical patterns of behaviour for people who regard things as 'sacred':

SITUATION 1: DOCUMENTS

For goodness' sake! I should have a secretary. Doing all these things at the same time – it's beyond my management ability. Flooded with client faxes every day, wads of documents every time there's a meeting and always having to check through past data and media reports. And at the end of a project all the papers have to be kept just in case. Oh no! I thought all that was rubbish, but it's important data. I nearly threw it out. It'll have to be distributed for reference at the next meeting.

SITUATION 2: MEMENTOS 1

She was such a cute baby. Look at this tiny thing she used to wear. They grow up so fast! Well, I suppose I'd better give it to the bazaar. The shawl's got some lovely lace, though . . . I think I'll keep it. And these baby clothes she wore when we went to the shrine – they were a present from my mother-in-law, so I can't get rid of them. Oh! Etchan loved this! She used to point at it and say 'Bear'. Everything's so full of memories!

SITUATION 3: MEMENTOS 2

The bookcase is getting too full. I'd better get rid some of some books. The problem is this shelf . . . I've kept all my books from university, but I'm sure I won't use them again. Maybe they'd be useful for work at the institute. Let's have a look. Wow! This takes me back. All that underlining! I took it all very seriously. Studied hard. Oh, what's this? Michiko 7pm. Shibuya – by the Hachiko Statue in Shibuya. Ha ha! Must have written that down while I was on the phone. Michiko! I wonder if she's married . . . Well, it's nice looking at these books from time to time . . . full of memories.

SITUATION 4: FOOD

The ham in the fridge has gone off. Again! What about this? Is this meat OK? All this milk – consume by . . . tomorrow! We've got to be more careful. Didn't your mother tell you not to waste food? Think of all the starving children in the world! And what about the farmers? Oh dear. I'm turning into my father.

SITUATION 5: BOOKS

You're getting rid of this? Throwing it out? You shouldn't do that. Books should be treasured. I get cross with the children if they don't respect books . . .

The 'sacred' mentality

The first thing I'd like to say is that you shouldn't automatically treat work documents as 'sacred'.

It may be unfair of me to quote a book on document management, but I am going to do so, because while the author fully appreciates the importance of getting rid of things in general, he treats work documents, and only work documents, as 'sacred':

> It is relatively easy to decide whether clothes, tools, food, etc. are necessary or not. If things are broken or rotten, then the decision is very simple. In general, the necessity or otherwise of something can be decided on

the basis of its physical characteristics or appearance. The subject of this book is mainly paper, and in some cases it is easy to make a judgement about this too. Used tissues or torn paper bags obviously serve no purpose. The decision is easy because they carry no information. There are certain types of information-carrying paper too about which a decision can quickly be made. For example, newspapers: once a newspaper is out of date it has little value and can probably can be discarded. But documents and memos are completely different. They can still be important, even if they are old and torn. Discarding important documents by mistake can cause extremely serious problems.

Yukio Noguchi, *Super-Organisation 3*

If you've read this far in my book, you'll realise that Noguchi's views are rather one-sided. If it was so simple to judge whether or not clothes, tools and food items were necessary, homes would not be flooded with things in the way they are. Ditto the workplace. The problem lies in the fact that so many unnecessary items are in useable condition. From this point of view, they're no different to documents. Anybody who can simply accept Noguchi's position is someone who already regards documents (= information) as sacred. It's this attitude that makes people incapable of managing the limitless flows of information we're all subjected to.

Many businessmen regard their work as the most important thing in their lives. They have little respect for things in the home, but treat anything to do with work as sacred. As long as they maintain this attitude, their workplace will always be cluttered.

The Art of Discarding is not limited to particular types of thing – it's an approach to life in general. Mementos, food and books are regarded as sacred for different reasons. Once you lose a body of information, it's difficult to rebuild. If you lose mementos they're gone for ever. Books are books and food is food, and both should be treated with respect. (I won't analyse why this is. Such attitudes to food and books are accepted as common sense. It can be difficult to show a clear basis for something, even if it seems reasonable.)

But whatever reason you have for regarding something as sacred, remember it's only you that is giving it that status. Nobody else regards it as 'untouchable'. The real reason you can't get rid of it is that you have some dependence on it.

Think like this!

To stop seeing things as sacred you have to tell yourself one thing: 'When I'm dead, it will all be rubbish.'

I don't want to criticise you if you think certain items are worth keeping. That would be as pointless as telling a believer that their religion is nonsense. You can file away papers that you'll never look at again. You can surround yourself with mementos and live in the past. You can let the floor collapse under the weight of books. You can forever be eating things just before their use-by date. And if you're happy like that, then that's fine.

But when you die, it will all be rubbish. If you were to die right now in a traffic accident, that album you've kept so carefully will be thrown away. Your books will be bought up as a job lot by a second-hand bookshop. Wouldn't it be better to clear things out instead and enjoy a clutter-free life while you can?

6

IF YOU'VE GOT IT, USE IT

A lot of things stay unused because they are reserved for guests, or for going out or because they form part of a set. But don't you think it's a waste to have something that you don't use?

Danger items

Books, magazines, CDs, tableware, clothes, etc.

When does it happen?

Once you start creating special categories, you often end up just 'having' things and never using them. The following scenarios will be familiar to everyone.

SITUATION 1: LOOKING AT A BOOKSHELF

I've loved Yasutaka Tsutsui's books ever since I was a student. Most of these hardbacks are first editions. I always buy the paperbacks too – for the commentaries. Then there was a complete works edition so I had to get that. He takes up the whole shelf. But it was his earlier works I liked best – some of the recent ones I haven't read at all. This one – I've never even opened it. I'll probably never read it. But I'll keep it. It's part of the set.

SITUATION 2: GOING HOME

Mum, I've brought a cake. Let's have some tea. Oh – you've bought a new tea service. Very nice! Let's use it. What? You don't want to? Just for guests? So what shall we use, then? What about these? The previous ones you had for guests. You don't want to use those either? They're just for your friends. OK. So we'll have to use the ones we've always used. Look, this one's cracked. Oh, Mum!

SITUATION 3: SORTING OUT YOUR CDS

These CDs are piling up. Perhaps I could sell some. World Music – that was popular. But I never listen to it now. I could sell all of those. Here's one by Queen. I used to like it. I don't think I'll sell it. All these by The Doors! I bought all their albums, but I only ever listened to these two. I could sell the rest. But then they're a set, so it'd be a pity. I think I'll hang on to them all.

SITUATION 4: OPENING YOUR DAUGHTER'S WARDROBE

You're going to a friend's house today, aren't you? What are you going to wear? Your red sweater with ribbons? No, you can't! That's for best. What about your strawberry one? No? You prefer the checked one? No, you can't wear that either. You've only worn it once. Keep it for New Year.

The 'have-but-don't-use' mentality

Dividing things up on the basis of use means earmarking some items as special. Once that happens, the 'special' items never get touched. Your treasure remains unused. Let's consider the mentality of keeping 'sets' and having things 'only for guests'.

Wanting a 'set' belongs to the collection mentality. A set gives a sense of perfection or beauty. I'm told that those who collect insects tend to focus on a particular species because not many people collect them or because they feel they can obtain specimens of every type. In the same way, if there's a set of fifteen books and you have fourteen, it seems a shame not to have the other one. This is only natural.

But once you have them all, there's not often much advantage beyond being able to say you've got them. If you begin to feel this matters, then you're venturing into the realm of the genuine collector. When you find yourself obsessed with completing a set, then you may be a lost cause.

The 'set' mentality can easily take hold for items like the works of a particular author or back-issues of a magazine. You end up with a choice of either keeping them all as a set or getting rid of them all.

The idea that things are more valuable as a 'set' is a dangerous one. You may be told by an expert that your plates were originally a five-piece set and, as such, would fetch a higher price. If you take that too seriously, you'll be under the spell of 'sets'.

And the 'for-guests' mentality is similar. The fact that people use 'sets' for guests reflects the idea that 'sets' are special. If teacups from a six-piece 'guest' set get broken and you only have four left, then they may well be stripped of their special 'guest' rank.

Think like this!

If you have it, use it. If you don't use it, don't have it.

Why should things be in sets? If you want to read a particular book, that book is all you need. If you're not going to read the whole set, why keep it? A complete set of books can look good, of course. But who besides you is ever going to look at your bookshelves?

Why bother to keep a 'guest' tea set for your friends? If you have cups you like, then use them all the time. Enjoy them yourself. Instead of having five for guests and five for ordinary use, just get five that appeal to you. It's cheaper and takes up less space. If you break one, you can always buy another.

Rather than acquiring sets, simply buy things when necessary. They'll come to feel like a set in due course. It's a more relaxed approach.

And don't bother to keep certain clothes for special use either. There's not much difference these days between everyday clothes and 'special' clothes, anyway. It's a waste to keep something as special and only ever wear it once.

$$\left(7\right)$$

STORAGE AND ORGANISATION METHODS
ARE NOT THE SOLUTION

Women tend to believe in and be keen on storage methods. Men like to believe in document-organisation methods. Things which are systematically arranged may look good and give the appearance of functionality. But the fact is that the first step in any effective approach to storage or organisation is disposal.

Dangerous places

This is a phenomenon affecting all storage places: wardrobes, food cupboards, tableware cabinets, shelves, fridges, bookcases, files, filing cabinets, etc.

When does it happen?

TV programmes often feature 'storage experts' who proudly expound their techniques for storing things. Such programmes are not as common as they once were, but they're still very popular, especially with women. Mail-order magazines, meanwhile, are full of adverts for storage goods. There are also floods of books addressing organisation of documents, books and computer files, which tend to appeal to men.

SITUATION 1: LOOKING AT A SALES CATALOGUE

A unit fifteen centimetres wide? Perfect! It would just fit in the space between the fridge and the cupboard. I could use it for those spices and sauces I've got by the sink. They look very messy at the moment. I could put some cookbooks there too. They'd be easy to get at.

SITUATION 2: WATCHING TV

Uh huh . . . So for the food cupboard it's best to have containers of the same size. Yes. They'll fit on the shelf best that way. And if you stick a label on you know what's what. That's easy. At the moment, I put everything in one big container, and if something won't fit in I shove it on the shelf in its bag. But then it gets damp. I'm really not much of a housewife. I wonder how many Tupperware containers I should get. I guess about ten would fit. Yes, I'll get ten.

SITUATION 3: OPENING A CUPBOARD

These containers are perfect. So well designed! The manu-facturers really seem to understand storage problems. The containers use the full width and depth of the cupboard. It's very neat. Even I've managed to get everything in. The row on the right is all towels. In the middle, underwear and pyjamas. On the left, scissors, tape, all that kind of thing. It's wonderful. There's so much space!

SITUATION 4: BACK FROM THE BOOKSHOP

Oh dear! I've bought all these books, and the bookcase is almost full. I'd better get another one – just for paperbacks. I'll arrange them by publisher; that'll be simplest. I don't think I can keep classifying hardbacks just by author. I think I'll have to divide them up like a library does: Japanese literature, foreign literature, social science, physical science, self-help and so on. Easy to find and easy to put back. Libraries must have good reasons for their classifications. So I'm sure it will work.

SITUATION 5: BACK AT YOUR DESK AFTER A MEETING

The piles of documents we get for meetings just get bigger and bigger. The trouble is everything's so easy to print out these days. Well, I'd better put this lot away. It doesn't really matter how many documents I get, though. I can handle them all with my new classification system. Very straightforward with this index. Look at that shelf. So tidy! 'Competence' – that's what it says. In fact, the whole desk looks like it belongs to someone else completely.

The 'storage/organisation-method' mentality

There are two potential pitfalls with these methods.

First, the methods are 'borrowed'. Experts in storage and organisation are generally people who enjoy such things. At the very least, they are temperamentally suited to it. This is what allows them to develop their approach in the first place. Your character is different to theirs. So however much you try to follow their methods, you're bound to fail at some stage.

People often say things like, 'I've tried all sorts of classification methods, but I still can't get my documents organised. I'm hopeless!' But this isn't just a matter of weak will. There will also be a mismatch between methods and character – the person can't use the methods without feeling uncomfortable.

What about curator and librarian systems? They seem designed with everyone in mind – can they be applied by individuals (as in Situation 4)?

Dealing with your own books is not the same as dealing with books for the general public or for a large institution. Libraries, museums and other organisations with large holdings have very systematic organisation methods and are run by professional librarians and curators. Think also of secretaries – they are professionals in scheduling and document organisation. All these types of work involve special skills acquired through dedicated study and/or experience.

But people don't often give these skills a moment's thought. Our storage and organisation methods are often random and therefore hard to apply. Looking back at Situation 2 (groceries) and Situation 5 (document classification), it's easy to predict that, before long, things will be back to how they were. To which you might well retort: 'So what about your so-called Art of Discarding? Is that any different?' I would say, yes, it is fundamentally different. Storage and organisation methods start from the premise that these are good approaches. At the moment, discarding things is generally thought to be wrong. My objective in writing this book is to break away from this assumption and also, I hope, to make you reflect on your whole attitude to possession.

That's enough self-justification. Now let's consider the other pitfall of storage and organisation methods, namely that we apply the methods without proper thought – that we'll classify things and then store them away without ever considering whether it's necessary to keep them.

This tendency can make life difficult for architects in particular. Let me quote a specialist:

Almost all homes have in-built cupboards and wardrobes. Women always insist on them at the planning stage. I've been asked to build five cupboards into a design so that the place will be tidy. But as soon as the family moved in all five were full and the house was still overflowing with stuff. People say it's common for animals to gather a lot of things together, hide them somewhere and then forget where they've put them. In mankind it seems to be women that do this (*author's*

note: male delusion). Women love cupboards and wardrobes because they can shut the door and keep things
hidden. We know from experience that they'll be happy
if the plans show a lot of cupboard space. But we also
know that however much cupboard space there is, it
will soon fill up as people buy more and more things.

Mayumi Miyawaki, *Houses for Men and Women*

Through my work I sometimes meet people from construction
companies. All of them say that houses with a lot of storage
space are very popular. Into this ample storage space go
storage devices. Into the storage devices go different types
of stuff, in accordance with storage methodology. And, over
time, the stuff accumulates. Looking back at Situation 1, we
can imagine small kitchen items being crammed untidily into
the narrow unit. And we can also predict that stuff will keep
on being stuffed into the cupboard in Situation 3 until it is
absolutely full.

Documents are no exception.

Think like this!

Storage and organisation methods must be viewed from a
completely different angle. We have to realise that these
methods are only necessary because there's too much stuff.
Reduce the amount of stuff and we won't have to rely on
these methods at all.

As Miyawaki indicates (above), the amount of stuff people

have is destined to increase until it fills the available storage space. People with too many books buy new bookcases. These bookcases fill up immediately, and again books start piling up on the floor and staircase. Whatever the size of your wardrobe, it will fill up with clothes. As long as you allow things to accumulate, you don't stand a chance of getting the place tidy just with storage and organisation methods. No organisation method can cope when there's not enough space to accommodate things.

Earlier I quoted Yukio Noguchi's *Super-Organisation 3*. The book was said to represent a radical new approach because of Noguchi's focus on the time dimension in the organisation process – good order, he argues, is not just a question of categorisation. But to me his approach seems similar to others in that it is still based on the belief that things can be organised if you follow a systematic methodology. Also, Noguchi proposes a provisional (or 'for-the-time-being') disposal buffer. I've already explained what would happen if such a stage is introduced.

Ultimately, I think the biggest danger of storage and organisation methods is that one may be seduced by the pleasure of preserving order. If the preservation of order gives you peace of mind, that is fine. But if you want to prevent things accumulating, it's important to employ really active disposal techniques.

If you reduce the number of things you have, then a system for storage and organisation won't be necessary. You'll be able to manage things naturally. Even if you leave them in a jumble, you'll be OK. I can understand people thinking that work documents are different. This may be true for academics, for example, who have to keep a lot of papers. But the number of documents someone like me has can be managed pretty well even if they're mixed up together.

I'm not a very tidy person by nature, so I don't manage my work room in a particularly systematic way. But on the whole I only keep documents that are essential, so I can always find what I'm looking for quite quickly. Knowing roughly where they are is generally enough.

Before finishing this section, I'll suggest one way in which storage and organisation methods can be useful. Let me quote a proponent of the simple life:

> I have read books and magazines about organisation techniques and storage methods. I tried a special storage method that said it would enable me to declutter without throwing anything away. But I found that I was just moving piles of stuff around and only making it look slightly better . . . So I made up my mind to get rid of everything that was unnecessary . . . I decided on this basis that 80 per cent of the stuff in and on my desk should go . . . Throwing things away is tougher than you'd imagine. Sometimes it makes you feel guilty. But you just have to think carefully, face those feelings, and carry on. That way you'll end up with only the things that are really necessary for you and your family. And because of the pain you've experienced discarding things you'll begin to

hesitate before buying new things too readily. I think you'll also begin to appreciate the feeling of taking care of things that are really necessary.

Eriko Yamazaki, *An Economical Life*

That is the message of someone who really thinks about her relationship with the things she owns. If borrowed storage methods have any use, it's simply to show us that they don't lead to a tidier house.

A final thought: we often come across methodologies that promote 'simple life' ideas from Britain and elsewhere. Yamazaki, for example, is basing her lifestyle on a German model. Her experience prompts us to think about how we relate to things. But I think it is best not to suppose we can easily introduce a different lifestyle from a foreign country. The fact that the expenditure-centred lifestyle of the United States doesn't work in Japan doesn't mean that we should look to another country for a model.

8

'MAYBE THIS COULD GO . . .'

This underlies each of the seven attitudes described so far. Whenever something catches your attention, whenever you start thinking about what it is or why it's there, always ask yourself whether you might discard it.

Danger items

Anything you see. Anything you pick up. Especially things that you normally wouldn't think were very important.

When does it happen?

It's a very simple idea. Look at everything from the point of view of getting rid of it. The following situations show the behaviour of people who don't have a discarding mentality.

SITUATION 1: SEEING AN ENVELOPE ON THE TABLE

I wonder what this is. It's open . . . The telephone bill break-down. The bill was bigger than I expected this month. Perhaps we should switch to a cheaper company like Tokyo Telephone. What's all this other paper in the envelope? Telechoice? ISDN? Guide to NTT Services? Perhaps the wife wants to have a look. It's been left here, so I won't move it.

SITUATION 2: A PILE OF NEW YEAR CARDS TUMBLES OUT OF THE LETTER RACK

They're all from last year. They've just been left here. Mm . . . a lot of these people I haven't seen for ten years at least. Oh dear, all these pictures of people's children. That's not going to cheer me up. Well, that was a waste of time. I'll put them back in the rack.

SITUATION 3: TAKING A GLASS FROM THE SHELF

Which glass to choose? I'm never sure, but I suppose this is the best for beer. Oh dear, I nearly knocked over the one next to it. I got that as a giveaway. It's got the name of the beer company on it, so I don't really like to use that. Still, I'll keep it just in case.

SITUATION 4: WORKING ON THE COMPUTER

It's good having the Internet. I don't have to go all the way to Kasumigaseki to see official statistics. I just print them out. For some reason it's much easier to look at figures on paper than on the screen – at least if you want to study them *carefully. Good. That's that. I'll file the printout. I may want to use the data sometime. It would be a pain to have to look it up again.*

SITUATION 5: STEPPING OVER A MAGAZINE ON THE FLOOR

Why's that in the way? I nearly trod on it last night too. Who put it there? Well, I'm the only one here so it must have been me. Last week's Weekly Asahi? *Have I read it properly? I'll put it on the table.*

Why we don't think of getting rid of things

Changing a situation requires energy. The easiest course of action is to do nothing.

If you see something, and it's what you're looking for, you'll pick it up and use it. You probably won't notice anything you're not looking for, unless there's a particular reason.

You'll notice some things just because they're in the wrong place – lavatory paper in the living room, pyjamas on a dining chair, your travel pass on the washing machine. Whether you actually put them back in their proper places depends on how tidy you are. But there are other things you'll notice because they look bad, redundant or in the way. These may be good candidates for disposal.

It's the same with things you pick up. Some will belong in a specific place, so you may just want to put them back there. That's fine. But if you stop and wonder for a moment what to do with something, then it's very likely that you could discard it.

All of the things that feature in the situations described above could be discarded – the telephone bill details, the New Year cards, the beer glass, the data printout, the magazine. If they were obviously rubbish, they would have been discarded straight away. But because they appear to have some value you forget that getting rid of them is an option.

Think like this!

The moment you notice something is the moment to get rid of it. If you don't, it may stay there for a long time.

This makes me reflect on just how good a custom the Japanese people have in the end-of-year clean-up. I'm not sure how it was in the past, but these days it's a major event – an occasion for getting rid of things that have built up over the year. Families clean everything inside and outside the house and throw away what they don't want. The clean-up makes us notice things and consider whether they can be discarded. The piles of rubbish in the streets at New Year clearly mean that thinking 'maybe this could go' is far from extreme.

9

DON'T WORRY THAT YOU'LL GET RID OF SOMETHING YOU SHOULDN'T

You may worry that you'll throw away something only to regret it later, and this might stop you in your tracks. But would you really regret it?

Danger items

There's an overlap here with things that are thought 'sacred' – documents, mementos, books, etc., but it happens with other things as well.

When does it happen?

Regret is probably the biggest fear for people who can't get rid of things. Let's think about situations where this fear is at work.

SITUATION 1: AT YOUR DESK

That's strange. It's not here. When did I do that job? Last year? But it's not in last year's folder. Those documents would help with this next project. What happened? Oh, I'm begin-

ning to remember. Yes. When I finished the job I thought I wouldn't use the documents again, so I threw them away. What a waste . . . I should never have got rid of them!

SITUATION 2: LOOKING THROUGH YOUR ADDRESS BOOK

Her address is still down as Osaka, but I'm sure she's moved to Kyushu. I remember throwing her letter away in last year's end-of-year clean-up. I thought I'd written her new address down. I got a New Year card from her, but I must have thrown that away too. How stupid! I can't contact her now.

SITUATION 3: TALKING WITH YOUR SON

What? You're planning to build something that complicated at school? Well, you've always been good at making things. Your teacher in Year 5 said she was very impressed. Your Godzilla was great. I remember that. What? You want to see it again? I wonder if we've got it. I'll ask your mum. Oh. We threw everything away when we moved. I'm sorry. We shouldn't have done . . .

SITUATION 4: AFTER TALKING WITH YOUR FRIEND

Gone out of print? I didn't know that. I should never have sold my copy. I didn't think I'd read it, though, and he told *me to sell any books that I didn't want. I only got about a hundred yen for it. I might have got a thousand for it now. Well, I don't want to be money-grabbing, but . . . Anyway, it's worth keeping a book that's out of print. I shouldn't always do what people say.*

SITUATION 5: AFTER TALKING WITH YOUR BOSS

Oh, how stupid! I didn't think there was any point in keeping that receipt from last week. He told me at the time that I probably wouldn't get it back on expenses, so I thought I'd have to cover it myself. Now he says there's an expense surplus, so I can submit the receipt, after all. I had a feeling it might be a mistake when I threw it away. It's so irritating!

SITUATION 6: ON A COLD WINTER'S DAY

It's been really cold today – as bad as Hokkaido. The ice didn't even melt in the city centre. What about tomorrow? What? Even colder? They must be joking! I hate the cold. Where's that padded jacket I had when I was a student? I thought I might wear it one day, so I put it away somewhere. 'Hey! Where's that old winter jacket I used to have?' 'I threw it away ages ago, dear. I checked with you first – asked if it was OK to get rid of it.' Oh, I remember now. I thought it was a mistake when she threw it away. I said I might want to wear it sometime and she said 'sometime' never comes. Well, it's come now, hasn't it?

The 'regret' mentality

If you throw away something important and irreplaceable, then, yes, there's a problem. So what sort of thing might this be? Can you think of anything straight away? A wedding ring, for example. Or something left to you by your father, which you intended to look after for the rest of your life. Or maybe a diary packed with engagements. Or your wallet. What about documents? According to Yukio Noguchi:

> Documents and memos . . . can still be important, even if they are old and torn. Discarding important documents by mistake can cause extremely serious problems.
>
> Yukio Noguchi, *Super-Organisation 3*

Is that true? I suppose it would be, if you really couldn't obtain another copy. And while a problem would arise if they were lost or stolen, they're certainly not the type of thing I'm suggesting might be deliberately discarded.

So what of things that we might consider discarding? Would we really regret getting rid of them? Let's look at the situations described above.

In Situation 1 some documents have been assembled and then thrown away. To get the same documents together again would involve repeating the original groundwork. And there's no guarantee that the data would all still be available. So it feels as though throwing the documents away was a mistake. But, in fact, old documents are seldom of any use. For people like me who use data a great deal in their work, documents that are even a few months old rarely have any application. This is because they are put together from the perspective of work being done at a particular time. The truth is that any documents that are really important would be ones that come to mind straight away. It's unlikely that there might be something useful in a pile of documents you have no clear recollection of.

The address book problem in Situation 2 is straightforward. You're bound to have a friend in common – you can ask them for contact details. Or you could ask the company she works for. It's just a matter of effort.

Situation 3, the child's model, relates to the loss of something that is valued for its associated memories. It's a question of 'sacredness', which I've already covered in Attitude 5. It's a shame, but if you took it too seriously you'd have to keep absolutely everything. Would you really want that? Parents have been criticised recently for taking videos of the whole of their children's school sports days or school shows. If they record it all, what are they left with? Is a memory no more than a recording?

The person in Situation 4 (the out-of-print book) may regret what she's done. But if you're not going to read a book and it's not that valuable, then I think getting rid of it is the right thing to do. And the person in Situation 5 is bound to regret the possible financial implications of getting rid of the receipt. But it's not the end of the world.

In Situation 6, it's a shame that the man wants to wear a

jacket that has been thrown away, but he didn't object when his wife suggested discarding it. And he might never want to use it again. The question is simply whether it would have been worth the jacket taking up space in his wardrobe for this one occasion.

Think like this!

If something seems a candidate for disposal, you're very rarely going to have a real problem if you go ahead and get rid of it. If it was going to cause a problem, you wouldn't even be considering getting rid of it. Think of examples from your own experience.

And don't worry too much about regretting what you do. Of course, there is a degree of uncertainty when making any kind of decision. But once you go ahead and start getting rid of stuff, I think you'll be surprised how little you regret.

(10)

DON'T AIM FOR PERFECTION

My final point is to take things easy. Over the previous nine points I've presented a kind of ideal. If you follow everything I've said, then you'll certainly be able to get rid of stuff. But even I can't claim to stick to all this advice all the time. Just take the points that feel right to you and implement them as far as seems reasonable.

Danger items

Anything that you find yourself worrying about regularly may find you suddenly wanting unrealistic changes.

When does it happen?

When you suddenly get enthusiastic about a new idea, or about making a change – it's easy to try to do too much too quickly.

SITUATION 1: READING ABOUT MANAGING A STUDY

Perfect – an ideal study! So functional. A real man's room. If only I had a room like that. I could enjoy being at home then. But with a house this size it's not possible. But why do the children have their own rooms while my study is just this little corner of our bedroom? Study management's not going to sort this place out. It's just piles of documents and books around a desk. If only the house was bigger . . . Ah well . . . This is all I've got.

SITUATION 2: A MOTHER VISITS HER DAUGHTER

Oh dear! Why are you so badly organised? Your sister's so neat and tidy. And people say I'm good at storing things too. In fact, none of my relatives is like you at all. Every time I come here, I find things all over the floor. Necessary? All of them? Well shouldn't you tidy them up a bit, then? Don't be cross! OK. I won't touch them. I certainly don't want to be blamed again if you lose something. OK, OK, I'm going. I do apologise, your ladyship. I was getting above myself.

SITUATION 3: ABOUT TO GO HOME FROM WORK

That office we went to today was so spacious. Everybody had a large desk and their own computer. It was like something in a TV drama. With desks that size, people can put all their documents away, so the place is bound to look neat. But here? Just one desk cabinet between two. Aargh! The pile of documents from the next-door desk has collapsed onto mine. He's so messy. But I shouldn't criticise others. I'm surrounded by great walls of documents myself. I can only *just manage to find space enough to do my work. If only they'd give us bigger desks . . . There's no point even trying to be organised with these.*

SITUATION 4: LOOKING AT THE TABLEWARE SHELVES

Full of stuff we don't use . . . I think I'd better sort things out a bit. 'The moment you notice something unnecessary, get rid of it.' Mm . . . OK. I'm going to get this done now . . . Mm . . . I've only got one of these plates left. It's a shame – I always tried to look after them. But there's no point keeping this one now. What about this bowl? We used it a lot for snacks with beer – put a bit of fish in there, it looks very nice. But he doesn't drink much these days, so we don't really use it now. I think I'll throw it. Oh dear . . . I've been at it for two hours already and I've only managed one side of the cupboard. I've had enough. I'm exhausted. I'll do the rest another time. Getting rid of stuff takes such a lot of energy.

The 'perfection' mentality

When I was talking about storage and organisation methods, I mentioned the danger of 'borrowing' other people's approaches. Everybody lives in a way that's easy for them. Without being conscious of it, we always choose the method that's gives us least trouble. We may feel that other people's values make sense, but it's not going to be easy to do exactly as they suggest – and if we try too hard, we're almost bound to fail.

In Situation 2, the daughter is discarding things in her own way, but the things she regards as necessary seem to be in a jumble. The mother doesn't like this lack of order. She wants her daughter to organise her house in a way that she regards as 'proper'. The daughter agrees that things should be done properly. But for her, disorder is natural. As far as actually getting rid of things that aren't necessary is concerned, she's doing as her mother says. But the mother is after 'perfection'. So the daughter gets cross and they have an argument.

As for Situation 1, anybody who is capable of keeping a study space neat should have managed it long ago in the corner available. This man's failure is not because of limited space. It's simply a question of not doing it.

It's the same with the person in Situation 3 and the piles of documents around the desk. Rather than hanker after the big desks she has seen in the other office, she should get on and halve the number of documents she has. But in my experience, if the difference between reality and your idea of 'perfection' is too great, you may lose the will to be tidy, and just allow things to accumulate.

The tidying of the tableware shelves in Situation 4 wouldn't be so bad if it was a regular day-to-day process. You open the cupboard every day, so whenever you notice something unnecessary just get rid of it. If you try to make everything 'perfect' in one go, it will tire you out.

Think like this!

The daughter who is happy with disorder cannot be the mother who wants order. Someone whose work space is the corner of a room will never be the master of a huge study . . .

To think about what to get rid of and how you relate to the things you possess – this, as I've said, is to really think about how you live your life.

Lifestyles have to allow people to be themselves. There's no point trying to do the impossible. What can't be done quite simply can't be done. Someone on an unrealistic diet will end up relapsing and wiping out any effect the diet has had. A weight regime has to suit you: give up sweet drinks, but keep on eating chocolate; don't limit your eating, but always walk to the station. In other words, don't aim for perfection. A regime that fits you may take a bit of time, but it's more likely to work.

Think of this as your 'stuff' diet.

PART TWO

Time to get rid of it

Ten strategies for discarding

DON'T LOOK – THROW!

D on't think: I'll have another look through and sort it out first. Get rid of it now.

What sort of things?

- Mailshots/flyers/adverts
- Pamphlets/catalogues
- Files/documents that have been stored away for a long time
- Books/magazines
- Letters and cards
- DVDs
- Clothes/household items you've been keeping in cardboard boxes, etc.

Strategy variations

1: DISCARD AS SOON AS YOU RECEIVE IT

- Mailshots/flyers/adverts
  Get rid of them straight away – when you open your

mailbox or when you find them inside your newspaper.

There's always a temptation to think that even obviously useless adverts may contain some information. Don't look. Just throw them. Only keep adverts that may be genuinely useful, such as information on a supermarket's discounts or a department store's mailing to account holders. Everything else should go.

- **Pamphlets/catalogues**
If you've acquired them on purpose, that's fine. But if you've been given them at a shop or they've been put through your letterbox, they should go immediately.

  If they look smart, you may feel like looking at them. Don't. You didn't want them in the first place, so just throw them away. There may well have been something attractive in them, but don't be drawn in – think yourself lucky not to have been tempted into buying something unnecessary.

2: DISCARD AFTER A PERIOD OF TIME (SEE ALSO STRATEGY 4 P.115)

- **Files/documents that have been stored away for a long time**
Are these really necessary? Don't start wondering if there was something important in them – just throw them away without looking. The reason they haven't been touched is because there's nothing useful in them.

- Books/magazines

  You bought them, read a little, then put them to one side. You may have thought you'd carry on reading them, but the fact that you haven't means they didn't interest you.

  Don't look upon a row of unread books as 'sacred'. Pick them up and throw them out. Don't even look at them. If you see a magazine lying around, don't think, Oh I might have another look through that. Just get rid of it. You may think you'll read it sometime, but you won't.

- Letters and cards

  People have put effort into writing letters and cards, so recipients often regard them as 'sacred'. And a lot of people enjoy reading old letters because they bring back memories. This makes them difficult to dispose of.

  But if you don't have a strong reason to keep a letter – if the associated memories aren't very important – don't feel you should hang on to it. Don't let yourself be put off throwing them away because they come from some-body important to you or because you might not have taken down an address. If you hesitate, the pile of letters will just build up for ever. You don't have to keep a hundred postcards just because one of them may include a tele-phone number that you haven't written down.

  Don't leave them in a box or in a letter rack, just chuck them all out. You're very unlikely to regret it.

- Clothes/household items you've been keeping in
  cardboard boxes, etc.

  Perhaps you put stuff in a box when you moved house
  and it's been in there for three years now. Maybe you put
  some clothes in a storage bin ten years ago, thinking you
  might wear them again sometime. Items like this are obviously unnecessary. The container you put them into has
  become like a 'black box' – you have no idea what's in
  it. Don't examine the contents – just throw them all away.

Why this strategy works

The key is simply in not looking.

It's natural to want to check whether something might be
necessary before getting rid of it. But this takes a lot of time,
and in the meantime other things are piling up. It's a task
that requires application and energy – deciding whether
things should be thrown out is tedious and tiring.

So for the kinds of thing I've mentioned above, don't
bother. Just get rid of them. Then it's all over in a second.
Things that were getting in the way are gone. It feels good.

$$\left(\,2\,\right)$$

CHUCK IT THERE AND THEN

Don't give your junk a stay of execution. Don't say 'someday', 'temporarily', 'for the time being' or any of that. You've got it in your hand – get rid of it now.

If the stuff is in a box or some other kind of container, open the container up first. If you don't open it, you can't really decide straight away. And leaving it as it is in the box is the most dangerous thing to do – it will be there for ever.

What sort of things?

- Mailshots
- Bills/statements
- Giveaways (novelties, calendars, etc.)
- Photographs (prints and negatives)
- Chopsticks, spoons, forks and sachets from takeaway meals
- Souvenirs, presents, seasonal gifts, etc.
- Damaged plates, pens that don't write well, blunt screwdrivers, etc.
- Electrical appliances, furniture, pans, tools etc. that you have bought replacements for

- Packaging
- Till receipts
- Work papers
- Magazines
- Leftovers
- Food past, or very close to, its use-by date
- Items in the fridge

Strategy variations

1: OPEN AND DISCARD

- Mailshots

  If it's your favourite brand or department store, you'll probably want to take a look. You open it up. You like what you see. You think, Wow! I wish I had that! You decide to keep the envelope for the time being . . .

  Stop! Throw it away there and then. It's nice to dream. But the fact is you're not going to buy the product.

  So just open the envelope, have a quick look and unless you see some really essential information inside, throw it away immediately without a moment's reflection.

- Bills/statements

  When you get bills for the telephone or a credit card, the envelopes always contain other bits of paper, advertising this or that. Open the envelope, take out what is actually necessary and throw the rest away immediately. Check through the breakdown of payments or calls then and there. Don't put it back in the envelope – if you do, you'll just end up going through the same process again later.

If you're worried about security, rip the paper up into small pieces and divide them between different rubbish bins, or use a shredder.

- Giveaways (novelties, calendars, etc.)
  It feels good to get something for nothing. If you really like it, then hold on to it. But if it's a question of 'keeping it for now', just let it go. It's important to take it out of its box or bag first, though. If you don't check the contents, you won't be following the process of 'open and discard'.

  If you don't want to throw it away, another option is to pass a giveaway on to someone else: if you've been given something at a fast-food outlet, give it to a child who'll like it; if you get a glass at a drink shop, give it to the sales assistant; if you get a calendar you don't much like, give it to someone at work.

- Photographs (prints and negatives)
  You've had some photos developed. Some are bad quality, others are OK, but of no particular interest, even to the people in them. Throw them straight in the bin. The moment you open the packets up is when you're going to be checking through them most carefully – so that's the best time to decide on throwing them out. And if you're not going to be making reprints, chuck the negatives out too. It will be difficult to check those later to see what's

in them, and they'll end up being put away somewhere, despite being no use to anyone.

- **Chopsticks, spoons, forks and sachets from takeaway meals**

  Some people who keep such items may actually use them, but others just hoard them in a drawer. If that's what's likely to happen in your case, you're better off throwing them out as soon as you open the box.

2: DISCARD ONCE THEY'VE SERVED THEIR PURPOSE

- **Souvenirs, presents, seasonal gifts, etc.**

  Gifts are all about the act of giving. So as soon as they've been given/received, we could say that their function has been fulfilled. But you wouldn't want to get rid of a gift when the person who gave it to you is there, so better leave it until later . . .

  Of course, if you're given something you want to wear, display or use, then keep it. And valuable things like rings and watches can be sold.

- **Damaged plates, pens that don't write well, blunt screwdrivers, etc.**

  Things that you can still just about use are hard to part with. You'll replace them sometime, but until you do, you'll put up with them. But is it really more wasteful to replace something straight away than to put up with it?

When a plate is cracked, when a pen stops working well, when a screwdriver becomes blunt, carrying on using them comes at the mental cost of irritation. (Worse still is if you hang on to something after you've obtained a replacement – see below.)

- **Electrical appliances, furniture, pans, tools etc. that you have bought replacements for**
  If you're replacing something because it's broken, then you probably won't hesitate to throw it away. But sometimes you might buy a replacement just because you like the design, or because it's more efficient. In cases like these, the old one may still be useable, and you may find yourself keeping it 'for now' or because 'it may be useful sometime'. But the truth is it will do nothing but take up space. You might also keep it because it costs money to have it taken away. But you'll have to get rid of it sometime, and you'll feel better if you do so straight away.

  If you intend to get rid of something, don't put it out of sight. If you do, you'll forget about it. Even if it's large and gets in the way, leave it somewhere you'll see it. Then you won't forget to dispose of it.

- **Packaging**
  People often hang on to boxes. They think a PC's box, for example, may come in handy if they move. Or they've received a parcel and think they might use the same box when sending something themselves. Or they've bought

a luxury brand product – the box is attractive and they think they might use it in the future.

But a box that was there to package a product loses its function once the product is taken out. If you want a box when you move, you can get one then. And keeping brand boxes is absurd. A pretty box full of air in the cupboard just occupies space.

Simply dispose of them.

• Till receipts

Some people keep records of every item of household expenditure. But for everyone else, till receipts are just something they're given. If you're one of the latter, don't put your receipts in your wallet or in your pocket. Throw them away immediately. Supermarkets sometimes have waste bins under the tables where you bag up. Many convenience stores these days also have places for you to throw away receipts. When leaving a café, keep the receipt in your hand and throw it away in a bin outside. Only keep receipts for high-value items that you may need to return, and period-ically sort through these, getting rid of any unnecessary ones.

• Work papers

As soon as you've finished a piece of work, decide whether to dispose of the related documents. Don't just keep them all 'for the time being'. If you find yourself thinking the documents may be necessary again 'sometime', refer to Part One, Attitudes 3 ('"Sometime" never comes') and 5 ('Nothing is sacred').

• Magazines

It's surprisingly difficult to throw a magazine away you subscribe to after you've read it. But as long as no one else expects to read it, dispose of it straight away. If you find an article you particularly want to keep, cut it out when you come to it. This will save you the trouble later. If you leave it until later, you're likely to have forgotten what it was you wanted to cut out. Make sure you get rid of your magazines before they start turning into a collection.

3: IT'S FOOD, BUT IT SHOULD STILL GO

• Leftovers

Readers may take me to task, but I would nevertheless like to suggest that leftovers can be thrown away. How many times have you wrapped up leftovers and put them in the fridge, only for them to go off? Or perhaps you've left food out until it's become dry and shrivelled.

When you have leftovers at the end of a meal, think about what to do with them. Don't just automatically put them in the fridge. Either eat them immediately or decide definitely to have them tomorrow. If you can't do either of these, then it's reasonable to throw them out. It may seem a waste, but it's the best thing to do. If you keep up this policy, you'll soon find yourself not throwing food away – either you'll have stopped preparing too much or you'll always eat the leftovers the following day.

- **Food past, or very close to, its use-by date**
  You think it's still edible, so you can't throw it away. But if you've kept it for so long already, are you really going to eat it 'sometime'? Now that it's got your attention, either eat it or, if that's not practical, throw it away.

- **Items in the fridge**
  Again, the important thing here is to take action as soon as you notice something: pickles, etc. you thought you were going to use but haven't; food that's near its use-by date; Tupperware containing – you're not even sure what. Take them out and decide there and then whether to eat them or throw them away.

Why this strategy works

'For the time being', 'temporarily' and 'sometime' are, as I said in Part One, phrases that reflect a natural human response. When we're troubled by a sense of waste, delay seems to make disposal easier.

But if you're going to get rid of something anyway, you may as well do so straight away. It will stop things accumulating, so there'll be less stuff to sort out at a later date. Just like summer-holiday homework, it's best to do a little at a time, rather than leave it all until later. And, of course, discarding things is easier than homework!

If you stop delaying disposal, you'll also stop diluting your sense of waste. Keeping a keen sense of waste – guilt at throwing things away – can have a very positive effect, especially when it comes to food. It may encourage you to think more carefully when shopping and when planning how to use your stocks. If it does that, then implementing the 'discard-there-and-then' strategy will have been worthwhile.

3

DISCARD WHEN YOU EXCEED A
CERTAIN AMOUNT

Set limits. The limit may be the capacity of a particular container – a bookcase, say, or a cupboard. Once your possessions exceed that capacity, get rid of anything that isn't required. Or simply decide how much of something you are likely to use – for example, wrapping paper – and don't allow your stock to exceed that.

What sort of things?

- Clothes, towels/sheets (cupboard; wardrobe); shoes (shoe rack); food (food shelves); books (bookcase);
- Pens, pencils (pen holder)
- Wrapping paper; string; boxes
- Used paper
- Pyjamas
- Bath towels, sheets
- Mugs
- Chopsticks, spoons, etc.
- Cloths
- Pots, kitchen utensils

Strategy variations

1: DISCARD WHEN THEY EXCEED A CERTAIN SPACE

- Clothes, towels/sheets (cupboard; wardrobe); shoes (shoe rack); food (food shelves); books (bookcase)
  Don't keep clothes on bedroom walls, in the corridor or the hall, etc. Decide on just one place to put them. Once that fills up, start checking through what you've got. If there's anything there that you never use, think about getting rid of it. The same approach can be taken with towels and sheets, with shoes that don't fit on the rack, food that doesn't fit on the shelves, books that won't go in the bookcase. Once you've decided on the amount of space each type of item should be allocated, think carefully before increasing it.

- Pens, pencils (pen holder)
  It may seem a minor thing, but it's worth keeping an eye on pen holders. They tend to fill up very quickly and you want to be able to take pens out and put them back with ease. So once this becomes difficult, get rid of some pens. It's likely that there are some that don't work very well, or others you were given but never use. Don't make the mistake of starting up a new pen box in your drawer.

2: DISCARD WHEN THEY EXCEED THE AMOUNT YOU CAN USE

- **Wrapping paper, string, boxes**
  It's good to have stock of nice wrapping paper, boxes, ribbons and string, which can all come in useful. But if the supply exceeds the amount you use, then stock just keeps accumulating. It should be easy to decide how much to keep, based on how much you use. Then you can choose a bag to keep wrapping paper in, say, and a box for ribbon, and once there is enough to fill the bag or box, throw away or recycle the excess. Deal with supermarket and department store bags in the same way.

- **Used paper**
  In the past people were careful to make use of the reverse side of flyers to write notes. But nowadays we have so much paper around us we can't regard it as 'sacred'. We have to consider throwing it away. Waste printouts can be useful for printing drafts or taking notes, but the amount you're going to use is limited. Decide how much you will actually use and identify a bag or file to keep that amount of paper in. If you exceed capacity, then recycle the surplus.

3: DISCARD WHEN THEY EXCEED THE NECESSARY NUMBER

- Pyjamas
- Bath towels, sheets
- Mugs
- Chopsticks, spoons, etc.
- Cloths
- Pots, kitchen utensils

For these and many other items it's easy to establish the number required based on how many are necessary per person. And don't allow for too many spares. It's important to have enough, of course, but the number you really require may be surprisingly small (see Part One, Attitude 6 – 'If you've got it, use it'). If you exceed that number, get rid of the older ones. Keep the same number over time, gradually replacing old with new. So, for example: three pairs of pyjamas (summer and winter), two sets of sheets, two bath towels, plus one or two for guests. As for mugs, spoons, pairs of chopsticks – one per person plus two extra for guests; cloths – four in total. Decide how many pots and serving plates you require according to size – for example, two large and two small.

Why this strategy works

We keep getting new things, but the old ones can still be used and we often hold on to them. This strategy provides an opportunity to get rid of the older things and so smoothes the replacement process.

This strategy works for many of those things that survey participants found 'difficult to dispose of'. Whether something gets thrown away or kept can depend on how many disposal opportunities you create.

4

DISCARD AFTER A CERTAIN
PERIOD OF TIME

Fix a suitable time period for the item – say, one month, one year, three years – and if it hasn't been used at all by the end of the period, dispose of it.

What sort of things?

- Manuals
- Catalogues, pamphlets, etc.
- Toys
- Documents/files
- Books/magazines
- Letters (including birthday and cards)
- DVDs
- Clothes, utensils, etc. that have been stored away in boxes or containers

Strategy variations

1: THINGS WHICH ARE ONLY USED FOR A LIMITED PERIOD

- Manuals

  We tend to buy manual-type books when there's a particular necessity – for childcare, cars, computers, computer games, etc. They're essential reading for people who haven't had exposure to specific tasks, and we may use them a lot to start off with, but then we may never open them again. If we do, it's just to check a detail or maybe for fun. It's seldom for anything crucial.

  So when you think your learning period is over, throw the manual away. After that, you can always look online or contact the manufacturer. There's no necessity to keep a large manual just on the off chance.

  A good way of disposing of childcare books is to pass them on to others who are having children.

- Catalogues, pamphlets, etc.

  It depends on the subject matter, but information in catalogues and pamphlets is often outdated after a certain time. Look for specific dates or periods that may be printed in one corner. It can be fun to look through old catalogues occasionally, but they're not going to be any real use. So get rid of them.

- Toys

  Toys that once absorbed a child will be used less and less as they get older. They tend to want to hang on to them for ever, so they're very difficult to throw away, but you can't allow toys to accumulate.

  Every year, say on or around the child's birthday, get them to decide what to throw away. As suggested in Strategy 3, it's a good idea to limit the space made available here by having a fixed-capacity toy box, for example.

  Sometimes you can dispose of toys by giving them to people with smaller children. But children often have a glut of toys, so this isn't always a reliable recycling method.

2. ITEMS YOU'LL BE ABLE TO DECIDE ABOUT AFTER A CERTAIN PERIOD

- Documents/files
- Books/magazines
- Letters (including birthday cards)
- DVDs
- Clothes, utensils, etc. that have been stored away in boxes or containers

All of these items were mentioned under Strategy 1 (see page 97). The basic idea here, however, is that if any of these things is essential, you're bound to see them at some point within a certain period – and if you haven't seen them by the end of that time, you should get rid of them.

I suggested in Part One, Attitude 3 that generally if you don't use something for three years, you don't need it, but you can decide on the periods most appropriate for different items. They don't always have to be worked out on a logical basis. The most important thing is for you to decide on a timeframe of some kind – the point being to create discarding opportunities.

Why this strategy works

Like Strategy 3, this creates a lot of opportunities to throw things away.

You set the period so that you won't just keep things for ever after you stop using them. Once the allotted time expires, you get on and discard them, no ifs or buts. You thought they might be useful 'sometime', but 'sometime' isn't coming. You know that now. In due course, you might get better at deciding fast what's necessary and what's not, and then you'll stop hiding behind those phrases.

If you think the period you have chosen is too short or too long (so that things are accumulating), you can always make adjustments.

$$\left(\begin{array}{c}5\end{array}\right)$$

REGULAR DISCARDING

Ask yourself regularly whether things can be thrown away. You can do this at the end of the day, week, month or year. In fact, you don't have to be too precise about the periods, just so long as you make the decision to do it with a degree of regularity. It could be just a question of thinking, Oh, I haven't checked for a while – then having a look and getting rid of anything unnecessary.

What sort of things?

- Receipts/despatch notes
- Household account books
- Spare buttons and keys
- Guarantees/contracts
- Product instructions
- Memos stuck on the fridge or on your memo board
- Stationery and other small items in drawers
- Ties, socks, underwear
- Books, magazines, clothes

Strategy variations

1: DOCUMENTARY RECORDS

* **Receipts/despatch notes**
  These are useful in case there's a problem with a product or delivery. (I'm ignoring here their use in recording household accounts or applying for expenses.)

  Once the products have been used or the delivery has been made, however, their useful life is over. Don't leave them in your bag or wallet. Every time you go shopping or open your wallet, get rid of any that you can.

* **Household account books**
  A lot of people like to keep records of day-to-day expenditure, and although they generally use a new account book each year, they tend to keep old ones. They can be good mementos, and it is surprising how often one wants to refer back, particularly to the previous year's accounts.

  So when you buy a new account book, keep last year's. But, at the same time, discard the one from the year before. Or, if you don't feel comfortable with this, keep each book for two years rather than just one.

  This regime of conscious, regular discarding means you will never accumulate more than a fixed number of account books.

2: THINGS THAT STICK AROUND EVEN WHEN NO LONGER NECESSARY

- Spare buttons and keys

  Spare buttons lie for ever in sewing boxes and drawers. Spare keys tend to be kept long after we've forgotten what they're for.

  When you throw away an item of clothing you're not going to take the trouble to seek out the spare buttons and throw them away too. So in due course, you'll have buttons that you don't want. That's why a regular check will help.

  If it looks as though you've accumulated a lot of buttons or if you have a lot of keys jangling about on a fob, sift through them to see if they're all necessary. Some of them will almost certainly not be.

- Guarantees/contracts

  Guarantees for electrical goods and furniture tend to last between one and three years. Contracts are often for between two and five years.

  When these periods are up, the documents become redundant. The best approach here is to keep all your contracts and guarantees together, then look through them on a regular basis. This might be at the end of the year, or perhaps whenever you put a new document in the file. If you then find one that has expired, you simply discard it. There's no difficulty deciding – an out-of-date guarantee is no use at all.

- **Product Instructions**

  Unlike guarantees, instructions don't have set time limits. But that doesn't mean we have to hang on to them for ever. Is it really worth keeping vacuum-cleaner instructions? And how long do you have to store advice on what to do if you think there's a problem with your heater or how to clean an electric fan or a leather jacket?

  There's a difference between manuals that can be used for troubleshooting and ordinary instructions we get with products. Don't confuse them. Once you've got used to a product, think about throwing the instructions away.

  Treat them in the same way as guarantees and contracts – store them all in a dedicated place. And whenever you put in a new set of instructions, check through the others to see if any can be discarded. Don't be tempted to keep them because they have the manufacturer's customer-service telephone number and it's a pain to make a separate note of it. If you don't have that specific number, you can always use the company's main telephone number and ask to be put through to customer service or simply look it up online.

- **Memos stuck on the fridge or on your memo board**

  Information on a sale or an exhibition, the school-lunch schedule, bills, telephone messages, a review of a book you're thinking of buying, etc. Any or all of these might be fluttering on the fridge door or a memo board.

Sometimes you knock one down as you brush past. When you pick it up you find that the sale is over or that you've passed on the message already or that the lunch schedule is for last month.

Make a point of checking through all of these whenever the space looks crowded or when something falls down. From my experience, one can always dispose of at least one third of the memos on display.

- Stationery and other small items in drawers
  Every household has one or two drawers where people shove miscellaneous items – stationery, nail clippers, unused films, compasses, spectacle cloths, etc. They might be in your telephone table, or your china or tableware cabinet. You may have a desk drawer at work which you use in a similar way.

  If you find these drawers easy to use, then that's fine. But do they sometimes get so full you have to press the contents down to shut them? If that happens, you need to sort out the contents. You'll probably find old memos, receipts from last year, pens that don't work, old snaps, a sticky, old sweet . . .

  Every time a drawer starts to look full, check through it. Otherwise, you'll always be having to push down the contents to close it. It may even jam shut, and exist only as a mysterious closed drawer.

3. WHEN IT'S DIFFICULT TO SEPARATE WANTED FROM UNWANTED

- Ties, socks, underwear

  A frayed tie, a sock with a thinning heel, old underwear – even if you notice them, it's difficult to throw them away. You tend to think you'll wear them just once more. Or some fastidious people may decide to wash them before discarding them and then once they've been washed, put them straight back in the cupboard.

  Get in the habit of regular checking. These are small items, so the overall volume won't be large, and they're surprisingly easy to throw away. It's up to you what cycle you set, but checking once in spring and once in autumn can work well.

- Books, magazines, clothes

  My survey suggests that books, magazines and clothes are the three things that people find toughest to discard. Creating more disposal opportunities must be a good idea. A system of regular disposal will not automatically make these items easy to part with. But I've listed them under this strategy just in case it helps you deal with them.

Why this strategy works

The previous two strategies involve disposing of things once they exceed a certain quantity or after a certain amount of time. This may be easier said than done though and things will still accumulate. So creating a regime of regular disposal will help.

Of course, it won't stop things accumulating between your regular clear-outs. And the more they do accumulate, the more onerous the regular checks will be. So this approach is particularly effective for items which accumulate relatively slowly, and when it's easy to identify whether they are necessary or not. Although I've included books, magazines and clothes in this section, please be aware that the strategy may not work very well with them if it's the only approach you use.

$$\left(6\right)$$

DISCARD THINGS EVEN IF THEY CAN STILL BE USED

Don't think you can't throw something away just because it can still be used. Change your mindset. Think to yourself, I've used it once, so I can throw it.

What sort of things?

- Clothes, books, magazines
- Cosmetics and toiletries
- Medicines
- Freebies
- Wrapping paper, string, boxes, used paper
- Spices
- Product samples

Strategy variations

1: THE BIG THREE – THINGS THAT PEOPLE FIND MOST DIFFICULT TO DISCARD

- Clothes, books, magazines

The approach here is basically the same as for items listed under '2' overleaf, but please note that people find things in these three categories most difficult to discard because it gives them a feeling of being wasteful: 'I can still wear it'; 'Maybe there's some important information there'; 'I haven't read it all'; 'It may be useful one day'. Almost everybody in our survey had this mentality.

The belief that things should be used until their potential is exhausted is a powerful one. People seem to think that if they keep something, there'll be the opportunity at some point for this potential to be used. (The reason some people like passing things on to second-hand shops is the idea that somebody else will take over this potential.)

But it's better not to bother about whether you use things to their full potential. It may well be the case that they could be used more, but they can still be disposed of. Accept this and you'll save yourself a lot of worry.

Or you could go a bit further and say, 'It's done what I bought it to do, so that's that. I've used it to the full.' Say you bought some fashionable clothes on impulse, for example, and you enjoyed wearing them once – that's enough. Or you bought a magazine for its special feature – you read the feature, so you don't have to keep the magazine because you haven't read the rest of it. In other words, by fulfilling *your* purpose, its potential has, in fact, been exhausted

2: YOU'VE GOT SOME YOU HAVEN'T USED, BUT YOU KEEP GETTING NEW ONES

- **Cosmetics and toiletries**

It is easy for make-up and toiletries to accumulate. And it's not just women that have trouble discarding these kinds of items. Men have similar problems, too. Not many women like to use the same eyeshadow over a long period, for example, so they tend to purchase new ones frequently. And even if you don't buy a lot of cosmetics for yourself, you may be given them as gifts. So you end up with a collection of partially used items.

Look in your drawers and baskets. Are there jars of foundation where you've reached the bottom at the centre but not at the sides? Are there tubes of hair gel that could be squeezed just a few more times?

Don't wait to finish them. If there's anything you haven't used for a while, simply throw it away. A regime of regular discarding (Strategy 5) is helpful here.

- **Medicines etc.**

There are various ways that this type of thing can accumulate. You may be given four days' worth of medicine for a cold, but take it for only three days and so have one day's supply left. You may buy something for a headache when you're out, even though you have painkillers at home. You may buy different ointments for various problems. Even if you think you'll be able to use them at some stage, once you've had them for a while you wonder whether you should.

Don't let these things pile up. If it's something prescribed by the doctor, throw any surplus away after you stop taking it. If you've got different boxes of the same type of over-the-counter medicines, and you bought them around the same time, combine them in a single box and try always to use that supply.

- Freebies
  Giveaways, like towels, soaps and tea, tend to accumulate. It doesn't seem right to throw a new towel away, and tea and soaps can always be used, even if you don't really like them.

  The towels can be used as cloths; you might want to keep them until your end-of-year clean-up then, once they're dirty, throw them away. That way you get your cleaning done and get rid of the towels at the same time. Of course, you can wash a towel and use it again and again if you want to. But if you do that too often, the number of unused towels will grow.

  With things like tea and soap, open them up and see if you like them. If you don't, throw them away. If you keep them, you probably won't use them.

- Wrapping paper, string, boxes, used paper
  These were all mentioned under Strategy 3 – 'Discard when you exceed a certain amount'. This means accepting the idea that it is OK to throw things away without using them up.

3: THINGS THAT ARE DIFFICULT TO USE UP

- Spices

  Spices just sit there for ever. You might have used them only once, having bought them when you were trying out an unusual recipe or when a friend recommended them.

  If you're not used to a particular spice or flavour, it's very difficult to use a whole jar of it. Don't be tempted by an attractive container into buying too much. It might look good on the shelf, but your kitchen has far too much stuff in it already. It's more sensible to get a small bag or sachet. And if it's not going to be a regular feature in your cooking, get rid of it.

- Product samples

  When you're out shopping you're often given free samples – perfume, shampoo and so on. It feels good to get something for nothing. But do you ever use these things? Perhaps you try them and then, if you don't particularly like them, you throw them in a drawer and forget about them.

  If you don't like them, just throw them away. Or, depending on what the product is, it may be good to take on a trip. Use as much as you need while travelling and then dispose of it while you're away.

Why this strategy works

With the 'I've-used-it-once-so-I-can-get-rid-of-it' mindset a lot of things are easier to discard. Depending on the item, it may be a question of 'once' or 'this much', but either way this attitude will stop you worrying about being wasteful. The approach basically emphasises disposability.

This is a slight digression, but the Western custom of making patchwork from old clothes can be helpful with this strategy. You may have clothes which you don't want to throw away because of associated memories. If you keep patches of material from them, it is less difficult to part with the clothes. You can then use the pieces to make a bag, oven glove or bed cover – whatever your handiwork skills are up to. A lot of people in Japan already use this approach with children's clothes, sewing patches together to make things like shoe bags for their children to use at school.

Perhaps it's a very female idea, but if you think that using one part of something may help you feel that the whole hasn't been wasted, then why not give it a try? On the other hand, if you end up with ten oven gloves in the house, you're just accumulating something else, so only try this idea with clothes that you find very difficult to throw away.

You might, for example, like to make a purse or a bag from a kimono or dress your mother used to wear. Changing form and reducing size – it's another method of disposal.

7

ESTABLISH DISCARDING CRITERIA

'Sometime', '. . . when I've used it as much as I can', '. . . when it's no longer necessary'. We've talked about these, and they are all too vague. They just don't work as criteria for disposal.

On the other hand, '. . . after three years', '. . . when I've used it once', '. . . if I buy a new one' – these are much clearer. Using periods of time, number of uses, etc. leaves no room for emotion and so facilitates quick, clear decisions.

Strategy variations

1. Decide on an amount
2. Decide on a time period
3. Decide on a number of times
4. Discard when you buy a new one
5. Have clear criteria for specific types of items
6. Review existing criteria

1. DECIDE ON AN AMOUNT

Establishing an amount as a basis for disposal was discussed under Strategy 3 (see page 110 for further details relating to particular items).

You should set a maximum amount of space (a particular cupboard, box, etc.) to allocate for different types of item. When clothes start poking out of the wardrobe, for example, then you should be thinking about disposal.

Alternatively, instead of space, you could think in terms of numbers of items. For example, you may decide to have three pans – one large, one medium, one small. If there's any more than that, get rid of the surplus.

2. DECIDE ON A TIME PERIOD

This approach was discussed under Strategy 4 (see page 115), whereby items are disposed of when the period elapses. This is obviously very suitable for things that are only used for a limited time, such as manuals, etc. It can work well for other documents too – the time period will allow you to judge whether the documents are necessary or not.

The first step is to acknowledge that things have a limited period of usefulness.

3. DECIDE ON A NUMBER OF TIMES

This was discussed under Strategy 6 (see page 126): instead of thinking you have to use an item until it gives out, decide on the number of times you should use it. When you reach that point, you can dispose of it. For many items 'once' may be an effective basis. Free hand towels or T-shirts, hotel toothbrushes and combs, product samples, etc. – tell yourself that you can dispose of such things after just one use.

4. DISCARD WHEN YOU BUY A NEW ONE

This is similar to fixing an amount. When you replace an item – TV, mobile phone, PC, briefcase, mug – dispose of the old one immediately. You had the right number until now, so unless you discard the old one, you'll have more than necessary.

5. HAVE CLEAR CRITERIA FOR SPECIFIC TYPES OF ITEMS

Things like clothes, crockery and magazines accumulate quickly, but aren't easy to throw away. It's tedious to go through them and decide what to keep and what to dispose of. So it's best to set clear criteria by type, so that you can decide straight away. If your box of carrier bags is overflowing, then tell yourself, for example, that you will keep all branded bags and throw away all department store bags away. To control accumulation of drinking glasses you've been given, you could decide to throw away all those that carry a company's logo. Magazines pile up quickly; you might decide to keep *National Geographic* for its beautiful pictures, say, but discard all others after a specific period of time.

There must be no ambiguity in the disposal criteria. As

soon as you see the objects, you should be able to decide whether they meet the criteria or not. And be careful not to give special treatment to items 'for guests' or items which are part of a set.

6. REVIEW EXISTING CRITERIA

Everybody already has some kind of vague disposal criteria. But if things have been accumulating, then these are clearly not effective, so you need to rethink them. Just becoming more conscious of what your existing criteria are will be a good first step.

Why this strategy works

Simple criteria like 'I'll throw out any clothes that no longer fit' or 'I only need three pots – small, medium and large' are enough to keep you on top of things. Vague and complex criteria make decisions tedious and difficult, and the purpose of this strategy is to eliminate this kind of problem.

When discarding something that can still be used, remind yourself of your commitment to your criteria. This may help you not to feel guilty.

8

HAVE PLENTY OF DISPOSAL ROUTES

Disposing of something doesn't have to mean throwing it away – it is simply a question of getting rid of it. You can sell it to a second-hand shop, pass it on to a brother or sister, give it to someone you don't know, or make it into something else and use it up. . . The more of these different disposal routes you have, the easier it will be to get things out of your life.

What sort of things?

- Batteries, needles, etc.
- Dolls, soft toys
- Clothes
- Books
- Expensive branded goods and accessories
- Sweets, cakes, etc.
- Electrical goods
- Paper rubbish (documents, receipts, mailshots, etc.)

Strategy variations

1: THINGS YOU CAN'T PUT OUT AS RUBBISH

- Batteries, needles, etc.

  Of course the local authority will provide a service for the disposal of batteries, needles, etc. But chances are you don't know what it is. It's a good idea to find out, but you're likely to discover there's only a collection twice a month. In the meantime the items are still there.

  Check out the alternatives. Batteries are often collected at local libraries, large shops, etc. When you buy batteries for your camera, radio etc. the shop assistant will often change the batteries for you and dispose of the old ones.

- Dolls, soft toys

  Through my survey I was surprised to discover that many Japanese people find dolls and soft toys difficult to throw away because 'they have eyes' or 'they might curse you'. Anybody in Japan who feels uncomfortable disposing of dolls as rubbish could try a temple. Some Japanese temples, especially those that run pet cemeteries, hold special services for dolls. Participation would cost several thousand yen.

2: THINGS YOU CAN'T THROW AWAY BECAUSE IT SEEMS A WASTE

- Clothes, books and expensive branded goods and accessories

  A welcome alternative disposal method for these is selling them or giving them away. You can sell online or use second-hand shops and bookshops, pawnbrokers, notice-boards in a local-authority office or local hall, specialist magazines or 'For Sale and Wanted' in a local paper. If the idea that they're going to be used again releases you from feelings of guilt about waste, then these are good options.

- Sweets, cakes, etc.
  You may have been given cakes, sweets, pickles or boxes of fruit. If the alternative is leaving them to go bad, then get on and give them away. If you're working, take them to the office – if you put a box of dried or fresh fruit near the kettle, people will take them happily. Towels and cups may be useful at the office too, so take them in.

  If a friend comes round, you can give them some of the food as a present – almost anybody would be delighted to accept jam, tea or chocolates, etc.

3: THINGS YOU DON'T WANT TO THROW AWAY BECAUSE OF THE ENVIRONMENT

- Electrical goods
  In Japan, TVs, air-conditioning units, fridges and washing machines are subject to a recycling law, whereby retailers are obliged to recycle items when requested by their customers. The law tends to make people think they shouldn't treat such items as rubbish. But did you know that the cost is borne by the consumer? When you buy a

new fridge you are charged for the removal of the old one. Thinking about how these electrical appliances are recycled makes me very uneasy. It may well be better to pay the local authority to pick up them up as large rubbish items.

Of course, sometimes these items can be sold or given away. If you know someone who is moving into their own flat, for example, you could ask them if they want your old television. They may be very pleased.

4. THINGS YOU CAN'T THROW AWAY BECAUSE THERE'S NOWHERE TO PUT THEM

- **Paper rubbish (documents, receipts, mailshots, etc.)**
  Have you ever picked something up, decided it was rubbish, but then, in the absence of a nearby bin, put it in a drawer and left it there? A simple answer here is that the more waste bins and baskets you have, the more you will throw away. It helps you to discard things on the spot. For paper and other burnable rubbish have at least one bin in every room.

Why this strategy works

Having a variety of places and methods for disposal makes the process easier. Choose the ones that cause the least trouble and anxiety. For example, if you can't throw something away because of a sense of waste, then disposal via a second-hand shop might be the best option for you.

In reality, things often end up being thrown away by somebody else anyway. But don't worry about that, as long as your approach helps you to get rid of things.

9

START SMALL

Choose a compact area – a table top, a kitchen shelf or a washstand, say – and decide you will definitely not put anything there. Then keep your resolution.

Strategy variations

1. Decide on a place where you won't put things
2. Decide on a place where you won't store unnecessary things
3. Start with a place that's easy to tidy

Strategy variations in practice

1: DECIDE ON A PLACE WHERE YOU WON'T PUT THINGS

- The kitchen table
- On top of a cupboard
- On top of the fridge
- A washstand

- A desk
- On top of a shoe-storage box

Let's consider the kitchen table. When not in use a table shouldn't really have anything on it. It's a place for eating, not a place for putting things.

But is there any household where the kitchen table doesn't have anything on it? Newspapers, a mailshot, a clock, some medicine, family photographs, a vase of flowers, a bag of sweets, a toy . . .

Then, when it comes to eating, all these things are just pushed to one side. They're not cleared away.

Try deciding that the kitchen table is a place where you will never put unnecessary things. Even if other places are overflowing, you will not put things on the table. So put the newspaper in the rack; if you want to keep any information from the mailshots or flyers, stick them on the door of the fridge and throw the rest away. Put bags of sweets away in a box. Throw away that medication you've stopped taking . . .

The table top is a relatively small area, so the task is easily done. But it does require a little effort every day as a result of which you'll develop a clear idea of the selection process: putting away what's necessary and disposing of what isn't. The regular repetition will help discarding become second nature.

You'll also have a nice, clear kitchen table and a sense of achievement.

2: DECIDE ON A PLACE WHERE YOU WON'T STORE UNNECESSARY THINGS

- Specific drawers

  Your handkerchief drawer, your towel drawer, the top drawer in your desk – anywhere will do. Just take a small storage area and decide that you will never put anything unnecessary in there.

  And then it's the same as with the kitchen table above. If you find yourself about to throw a meeting file into your stationery drawer, stop. If you're about to put a receipt in the telephone table for safekeeping, don't. If a CD won't fit onto its normal shelf, don't just shove it in the drawer.

  If you manage to stop yourself dropping things into drawers too easily, you'll develop the there-and-then habit.

3. START WITH A PLACE THAT'S EASY TO TIDY

- Towel drawer
- Cosmetics drawer
- Hall cupboard

It's difficult to tackle the whole house at once, so start with a compact place used for things that are relatively easy to sort out.

Take the towel drawer, for example. First, think how many towels are necessary (see Strategy 3, page 110). Remove the excess number and decide there and then on how to dispose of them. If the drawer contains giveaway hand towels or sheets and toiletries which shouldn't be there, take them out and decide what to do with them.

You may find all sorts of things at the bottom of the drawer. As you clear them out, contemplate just how much unnecessary stuff is there.

Once you've had your test-run in a compact space, gradually expand your area of operation.

Why this strategy works

It can be tough suddenly to change one's habits. Discarding isn't simply about tidiness. It's a whole way of relating to things. If you say to yourself, 'Right! I'm going to put this Art-of-Discarding thing into practice now', the chances are that you'll be overwhelmed by the sheer volume of stuff you're confronted with.

This strategy helps overcome that difficulty. The point is to start with small tasks, rather than taking on a big job all at once.

I recommend that you first try to establish a place where you won't put things (Strategy Variation 1). It's easier to feel the impact if you're dealing with a place you can see.

The first thing you'll notice is how many unnecessary things you have around you, and how they increase in number day by day. As this begins to bother you, you'll want to do something about it.

By following this strategy you'll also develop the habit of

disposal – of reducing the number of unnecessary things you have. Instead of picking redundant things up and then putting them back, you'll pick them up and dispose of them. This is why it's important to start with a compact place. If the job is too onerous, you'll get fed up before discarding becomes habit.

But once you've seen the effect on a small scale, I hope you'll want to apply the Art of Discarding to all aspects of your life.

10

WHO DISPOSES OF WHAT? DECIDE
RESPONSIBILITIES

I f space is being used by more than one person, it's important to establish who is responsible for disposing of what.

In a home, for example, the husband might be given responsibility for post and newspapers, while the wife is accountable
for clothes, food and things to do with the children. An alternative approach would be to allocate responsibility by area,
rather than by item.

Similarly, in the workplace it's good to establish who's
responsible for the spaces beyond individual desks.

Strategy variations

1. Divide responsibility by items
2. Divide responsibility by area

Strategy variations in practice

1: DIVIDE RESPONSIBILITY BY ITEMS

- Newspapers, flyers, magazines; post (bills, mailshots,
  adverts, catalogues, etc.); books

Let's say a husband has responsibility for disposing of newspapers. This doesn't mean that he automatically disposes of every newspaper he sees. It means that when unwanted newspapers have been lying around for a while, it's up to him to get rid of them.

If, for example, there's a newspaper on the living-room floor and a couple hasn't fixed their respective responsibilities, then there may be confusion – each might think the other still wants to read it, or get irritated that they have read it but not thrown it away. Worse still, they may not even notice it, so that it lies untouched for days on end.

Allocating responsibilities averts this situation. In this case, the husband will wonder whether the newspaper should be discarded. He'll check the date and, if it's yesterday's, he'll ask his wife if she's read it. If she has, he can throw it away there and then. If she hasn't, he'll say 'Do you want to read it? If not, I'll throw it. If you do want to read it, then could you throw it away afterwards?'

Of course, if the wife notices a newspaper on the floor, she should be able to suggest throwing it away. She shouldn't feel it's nothing to do with her. But the main responsibility would be with the husband.

I have included newspapers, post and books in this section because responsibility for these items might easily be taken by anyone. Disposal of most things in the house is often down to women – clothes, shoes, socks, general household goods, etc. But I think it's a good idea to have at least some division of responsibility.

In the workplace, there are often a lot of people, so allocation of responsibility is even more helpful.

Take magazines for example: say A is responsible for weekly magazines and B for other magazines. In this role A has established a rule that all weekly magazines should be disposed of after two weeks. If anybody wants to keep one of the magazines at the end of that period, they tell A. They can do so by leaving a message to A in the magazine. If, after two weeks, A sees a magazine belonging to the company lying on someone's desk, it's his role to pick it up and dispose of it.

2: DIVIDE RESPONSIBILITY BY AREA

- **The kitchen table, the lavatory, the hall, the living-room table, the staircase**
  Let's say the husband has responsibility for the kitchen table (see Strategy 9, page 141). Whenever he looks at it, he'll wonder whether anything can be discarded. He may see his wife's credit card statement, some printouts from school or flyers from the morning paper, and he'll ask if they can be thrown away. This will be an opportunity to discard things that have been put there 'for now' and have no real purpose.

  In the living room, kitchen and other large, well used spaces, I recommend that responsibility is set according to category of item rather than place. Just as with the house overall, the burden of having full responsibility for these rooms is too great. The person will feel resentful and arguments are likely.

Why this strategy works

Making responsibilities clear will enable you to avoid situations where everybody thinks someone else will act, but nobody does. It takes effort to make and implement decisions, and people are only too pleased if someone else assumes responsibility. So they leave it, and things that should be thrown away stay put.

Issues of responsibility came up repeatedly in my survey: 'I'm living with my boyfriend now and some things that are necessary to him don't seem necessary to me, and vice versa' (female, aged twenty-four); 'Now I'm living with someone else, I can't just throw away things like credit card statements' (twenty-something female). In these cases, things proliferate because people think they don't have the right to discard them. Another respondent had no such problem with her husband's things, however: 'When you marry, you've suddenly got twice as much stuff around you. I have no problem discarding other people's things, but I can't throw away my own' (female, aged forty). (This last example reminds me of myself when I got married!)

All of these people would benefit from clarification of responsibility. The first two would then have the right to ask if they can throw something away, while the third would be encouraged to think she must discard her own things in the

same way that she discards her husband's. Dividing responsibility in the home by room can help to avoid disputes, as
the person who has responsibility for the room in question
clearly has the right to ask about anything in it.

But I'd like to express just one important caution for the
sake of a peaceful life: don't be too interfering.

PART THREE

How to feel better about getting rid of things

Alternatives to throwing away

In this last part I will provide some information that may help you to dispose of things without feelings of resistance or anxiety.

So far, I've encouraged you simply to dispose of things, introducing you to attitudes and strategies that will help you. I've mentioned various methods, including throwing away, recycling, selling, etc. And, as I said under Strategy 8 (see page 136), throwing away and recycling are the same in that they both get rid of things. This has been my basic stance.

That said, it is tough to throw things away when you're thinking that it's a waste, or that perhaps someone else could use the item. It's sad for the thing itself. So at this point I'd like to say that throwing things away is the most extreme in the range of disposal methods.

We can dispose of anything by throwing it away. It may cost some money, but if you feel no resistance, throwing things away is easy. Before throwing things, though, there are plenty of other methods of getting rid of them – methods which many people may find more appealing.

I have tried to identify methods that anybody can use. In doing so, I have focused on things that people find difficult to dispose of, and on things that people want useful information about. I have also gathered some information that might allow people to throw things away more readily. I would like to share some of that with you and hope that it will help make disposal an easier process.

WHAT INFORMATION DO PEOPLE WANT?

First, let's consider what information people want about disposal methods. In the 'Can't-discard' survey described in the Introduction, my last question was: 'What information do you want about disposal?' Over 20 per cent of respondents (twenty-eight people) said they wanted to know about the reuse of items. Within this category, the information required ranged from the very general to specific points on particular types of reused items, second-hand shops, flea markets and how to make the sale, donation or recycling of second-hand items go smoothly. It seemed that many people want things to be reused where possible.

Ten people wanted to have information about garbage disposal. More specifically, how to separate it, services that take things away for no charge, how to dispose of personal information, etc.

Eight people wanted to know about storage and organisation methods. They seemed to think this might lead to more space being available and, therefore, relief. I would suggest that these people read Part One, Attitude 7: 'Storage and organisation methods are not the solution' (see page 71).

FEELING GOOD ABOUT DISPOSAL OF BOOKS

Methods of obtaining and keeping information have changed considerably in recent years. Although the focus now is not so much on having information as on how to use it, the feeling remains that information shouldn't be wasted.

Let's look at books, leaving aside the love of books as things to collect, and talking about them as information. I believe it is time to stop overestimating the value of the contents of books. This, of course, includes fiction and images.

If the content of a book is essential, then you can generally assume you'll be able to obtain it again – via the Internet for a start. So you don't have to worry that a book you dispose of may 'sometime' prove necessary. And for people who can't dispose of books out of a sense of waste, there are charitable organisations that will take them, as well as the traditional second-hand book shops. Why not give them a try?

Some ways to dispose of books

The following are useful methods of book disposal:

1: SELL TO SECOND-HAND BOOKSHOPS

Not all second-hand bookshops deal in books that are old

and valuable, so you might be able to find one that would be interested in what you are selling. Books usually have to be in good condition. Even if there are some books among those you take in that they deem valueless, they may still take them all.

2. SELL TO INTERNET BOOKSHOPS

An Internet search 'second-hand bookshop', 'second-hand book' or 'old books' should throw up a lot of options. Many have been set up by individuals, others are existing second-hand bookshops that have expanded online.

To find a suitable shop, look at what you have to sell. If there's a match between the books you have and the type sold by a particular second-hand bookshop, approach that shop.

Next, confirm online whether the books will be accepted. Some sites run by big bookstores will not buy. Those run by individuals are more likely to do so.

3. AUCTIONS/FLEA MARKETS

Internet auctions get a lot of attention these days and the number of people using them is growing rapidly. It's easy to take part, so why not have a go (see page 162 for details)? It's a nice feeling if books you've looked after go for a good price, and if you don't find a buyer, then throwing them away will be the inevitable choice.

4. LIBRARIES

Many local libraries will accept donated books, although different ones will have different policies, so it's worth telephoning first to enquire, so that you don't find yourself having to carry a heavy load home again.

As mentioned above, there is also the option of selling to second-hand bookshops, which still has an attraction for people who love books. It's a wonderfully satisfying feeling to find a bookshop that wants your books.

FEELING GOOD ABOUT GETTING RID OF CLOTHES

A lot of people donate clothes to second-hand shops or sell them ast boot fairs or flea markets. Many second-hand shops stock valuable designer items and appreciate donations. This is useful if you have a quantity of clothes, and don't want money for them, but don't like the idea of throwing them away.

Ways to dispose of clothing

The following are useful ways to get rid of clothes:

1: CHARITY SHOPS

Most high-street charity shops will accept second-hand

clothing. You can take your unwanted clothes to the shop yourself, or some organisations will post bags through letterboxes and then collect them on a specified day.

2: RECYCLING

Local-authority recycling centres usually have bins for unwanted clothing. There are also companies that will collect clothing from your home for recycling, some of which will pay for them.

3: SECOND-HAND SHOPS

In addition to donating, selling is also an option. Second-hand shops can be located both on the high street and online. An internet search will tell you what's available in your area, as well as directing you to websites where you can sell online.

FEELING GOOD ABOUT DISPOSAL OF ELECTRICAL APPLIANCES

Electrical items can often be tricky when it comes to disposal. Here are some ideas:

Domestic appliances

Home electricals will usually sell in second-hand shops up to a maximum of three to five years from original purchase as long as they are in good working order. For telephone chargers the cut-off is about two years, while for fridges and washing machines it's about three. (If you live alone and don't use the washing machine much, it might have a life of up to five years.) Televisions are OK if they work properly, but it's best for them to be less than five years old.

For machines that are easy to use, such as a fridge or washing machines, it is OK if you don't have the instructions. For more complicated TVs, telephones or music systems, the price offered will probably be lower if you can't supply instructions.

Personal computers

PCs and related equipment are often sold between individuals over the Internet. If a seller has what a buyer is looking for, a good price may be paid. So it's worth considering putting your PC into a flea market or auction. But this kind of trading is best for people who have a certain amount of knowledge, so if you're a beginner you may feel more secure going to a second-hand shop or consulting PC magazines.

People may be concerned that their PC will have personal information on it when it is disposed of, but as long as you erase the data properly you should not have to worry about disposal.

Lastly, recycling is again an option for disposal here. The local authority recycling centres provide an area where PCs can be dumped.

DISPOSING OF ELECTRICAL APPLIANCE
GUARANTEES, INSTRUCTIONS, ETC.

Electrical products come with a lot of documents. They look important, so it takes courage to dispose of them. But if you're going to just use the product yourself, there's not much call for them.

Guarantees

If you lose your guarantee, some companies will still honour its terms. They will check with the retailer when the appliance was sold and therefore whether it is still within the guarantee period. If the guarantee period is over, it's possible that the company concerned will mend your appliance for a fee. But either way, there is no necessity for you to keep the guarantee for ever.

Instructions / manuals

There is no problem if you throw these away. Most manufacturers have websites and if you look there, you will find information about how to use their products and related accessories, etc. If your product is still in circulation, it is likely that you will find any necessary information on the Internet.

People who don't like using the Internet can telephone the company. They will give you detailed advice. Many have free customer support helplines and they'll tell you what's in the instructions, or give advice on basic aspects of use. They might even offer to send you the relevant information.

It's probably advisable, however, not to dispose of the basic operating instructions for a PC. When you talk to the support centres they often respond with reference to the manual – for example: 'Look at page X of the instructions'. But if you do happen to lose (dispose of) the manual, they will still handle your queries, and may offer to send you photocopies, so you don't have to worry.

Boxes/packaging

When sending a PC in for repair or when moving house it's not necessary for it to be transported in its original packaging. The fact that the box is exactly the right size doesn't mean that it is especially effective in protecting against impact. Removal companies may say it's best to have the same box, but they are just playing safe. Any cardboard box of the right size will do.

FEELING GOOD ABOUT DISPOSAL IN GENERAL – INTERNET AUCTIONS

When you want to recycle or sell something there are various steps you can take: ask the local authority, put it into a local flea market, sell it to a second-hand shop, have a garage sale . . . These methods are well known and relatively easy to implement. You can find plenty of information about them on the Internet, using keywords like 'flea market', 'personal sale', 'auction', 'recycle', and by adding other words, such as 'books', 'children's clothes', 'branded goods', 'toys', 'cars', 'PCs', you can narrow your search. You can find anything. There are also a lot of specialist magazines.

At this point I would like to mention Internet auctions, which have become increasingly popular. One of the best-known is eBay which, in addition to operating auction-style sales has also expanded to include 'Buy It Now' shopping. There are also more specialised sites that might be of interest. You can search for them online, and once you access them you'll find a summary of their services and how to use them.

If somebody wants something that you want to get rid of, an Internet auction may allow you to find that person. It is a very good solution for people whose sense of waste won't let them throw things away.

If this kind of recycling becomes part of our society's system, it will mean that things can circulate. This circulation will prevent things accumulating in people's homes, so that there will be less *stuff* in society as a whole.

FEELING GOOD ABOUT THROWING THINGS AWAY

If we end up choosing to throw something away, we all know that we have to assign it to a particular class of rubbish.

Local authorities provide different bins for different items, but these don't cover all everyday items.

Recycling items are often easy to classify – plastic bottles, glass jars, cans, newspapers, etc. But not everything is easily categorised. Of course, local authorities will deal with matters in different ways and the management will vary according to where you live. It is important that individuals are well informed as to the local rules and that they follow them. One urgent task is to reduce overall volumes of rubbish through effective collection of recyclables. In terms of the handling of different categories of non-recyclable rubbish, the greatest problems relate to waste-plant capacity and collection systems.

THE RECYCLING TRAP

Finally, I want to talk briefly about the dangers of wanting to pass things on for reuse or recycling.

At worst, the desire to see things reused can lead to the simplistic thought that someone will use it eventually . . . This way of thinking allows people to buy things that are unnecessary in the belief that there's no waste – if they don't want it, someone else will. This leads to a vicious cycle of purchase and disposal: things accumulate, you pass them on, then more things accumulate. And what you believe to be a waste-free method of disposal often ends up with some-body else simply throwing things away on your behalf.

The media has highlighted many examples of recycling

systems failing to cope with the resources collected. Also widely reported in Japan are the problems of relief organisations being inundated with unwearable clothes, torn futons, tatty old blankets and more in the name of 'charity'. This problem is not now as great as it once was, but it has not gone away.

It seems to me that the recycling that individuals can achieve and the development of a societal system of recycling are two different things. A book called *To live an environmentally friendly life we must not recycle* by Kunihiko Takeda examines the burden that recycling of things like paper and plastic bottles places on the environment. I do not entirely agree with the author in every aspect, but I do subscribe to the idea that individuals cannot build environments on their own, that recycling can be very inefficient and that burning of waste may often be a better option.

But I shall leave to the experts all questions of whether we should have a 'recycling society' and how it might be achieved. What I want to emphasise for now is the message: 'start by disposing of things'. This is because, as I have pointed out already, the difference between disposing as rubbish and disposing for reuse is little more than emotion.

The first thing each of us should do is dispose of the piles of things that surround us. This will help change the way we live. And perhaps that could lead to changes in the way businesses and the rest of the country function.

Afterword

I have worked in marketing since the late 1980s. The purpose of marketing is to support companies' product development and advertising activities by probing consumer mentality and behaviour. In other words, I've been involved with techniques for making people buy stuff.

The late 1980s was the peak phase of Japan's bubble economy. The distribution industry was growing fast and manufacturers were working hard to develop new products. As the country entered the recession of the 1990s I heard first-hand from manufacturers about their wish to find hidden demand, from companies that saw opportunities in environment-related business.

At a time when companies were frantically trying to make us buy, had we stopped buying? I think the desire to buy was still there. But there were certainly fewer things that *everybody* wanted. It was no longer a question of everybody wanting the same thing. People already had basic consumer goods. Demand was now more individual. I think this marked a shift in the relationship between 'things' and 'self'.

Modern housing, furniture and appliances have made our

lives easier than in the past. But how many people are living in homes where they can relax and be themselves? Homes are crowded out with things. People can't find space for themselves. They want to find new ways of making their homes more pleasant to live in.

This book did not develop on the basis of a specific plan. Rather, I would say it has grown from my struggle to understand our relationship with things. I have tried to propose attitudes and strategies for the Art of Discarding based on my own experience and research, rather than on any clearly established social phenomena or statistics.

I have worked with the book's editor, Kayano Nemura, on various projects over many years. Once I told Kayano my ideas for this book, it did not take long for it to take shape. Things can proceed remarkably smoothly when one is working with a kindred spirit, and the publication process was a very happy experience. I am very grateful to the publisher, Takarajimasha, for publishing this book and for the speed of their decision to do so.

About the author

Nagisa Tatsumi was born in 1965. After graduating from Ochanomizu University, she worked as a journalist and editor before going freelance. Her writing focuses on Japanese lifestyle and culture, and her no-nonsense style has earned her a devoted readership. In 2008 she set up Kaji Juku, a training school for homemakers in Tokyo. Since 2016 Tatsumi has been the Director of the Lifestyle Philosophy Institute. She has written several books, many of which have been translated.

About the translator

Angus Turvill is an award-winning translator. His publications include *Tales from a Mountain Cave* by Hisashi Inoue (set in the tsunami-affected region of Japan) and *Heaven's Wind*, an anthology of fiction by contemporary Japanese women writers.